Constraint Grammar - Methods, Tools, and Applications (CG-MTA 2023)

Thorshavn, Faroe Islands
22 May 2023

ISBN: 978-1-7138-9060-7

Printed from e-media with permission by:

Curran Associates, Inc.
57 Morehouse Lane
Red Hook, NY 12571

Association for Computational Linguistics
209 N. Eighth Street
Stroudsburg, Pennsylvania 18360

Phone: 1-570-476-8006
Fax: 1-570-476-0860

acl@aclweb.org

Additional copies of this publication are available from:

Curran Associates, Inc.
57 Morehouse Lane
Red Hook, NY 12571 USA
Phone: 845-758-0400
Fax: 845-758-2633
Email: curran@proceedings.com
Web: www.proceedings.com

CG-MTA 2023

Constraint Grammar – Methods, Tools, and Applications

Proceedings of the Workshop

May 22, 2023

Association for Computational Linguistics (ACL)
209 N. Eighth Street
Stroudsburg, PA 18360
USA
Tel: +1-570-476-8006
Fax: +1-570-476-0860
acl@aclweb.org

Editors: Eckhard Bick, Trond Trosterud, Tanel Alumäe

Preface

The Constraint Grammar Workshop at NoDaLiDa goes back to 2007 and is the main regular venue of the Constraint Grammar community, bringing together researchers from not only the Nordic region, but also eliciting interest from other countries. With the exception of the Covid year 2021, the workshop has been arranged at every NoDaLiDa since its inception, making it the eighth one in a row. The workshops have focused both on theoretical issues linked to the Constraint Grammar framework and on it uses in the detailed analysis of natural languages at various linguistic levels. In addition, contributions about Constraint Grammar-based applications have played an increasing role, with a growing number of papers dedicated to this area.

This tendency towards applications and real-life integration has been especially clear in the current edition of the workshop, that had an overweight on CG-based practical programs targeting proofing tools. Thus, 4 papers presented work on grammar checkers, covering *Faroese, Inari Saami, Lule Saami and South Saami.* All papers focused on a restricted set of error types, but in each case the error types represented high-frequency problems in the language in question. The Faroese contribution was about errors related to the letter ð in morphological suffixes, for Inari Saami the focus was on a specific set of interference errors from Finnish, while the Lule Saami article presented the broadest set of error types, with agreement phenomena being the common denominator. The last grammar checker paper, about South Saami, looked at two problematic parts of the grammar, adjective agreement and negative constructions. All four grammar checkers represented finished and tested work for the error types in question and were released during the workshop.

A further two papers presented applicative, CG-based programs, where a down-stream, higher level NLP task was solved using a dedicated Constraint Grammar rule set. Thus, the paper *Attribution of Quoted Speech in Portuguese Text* exploits new Constraint Grammar techniques dealing with long-distance relations, such as co-reference links spanning several sentences and the dynamic use of stream variables, to automatically annotate news and literary text for quoting and attribution constructions, using syntactic, semantic and pragmatic tags as clues to identify and classify these constructions and to link them to specific speaker IDs. Another applicative contribution was an ICALL paper that used Constraint Grammar for the automatic scoring of learner essays written in *Basque*, with scores expressed in terms of the European framework CEFR for language level assignment.

Finally, a more theoretical paper, *WITH Context: Adding Rule-Grouping to VISL CG-3,* addressed the CG rule formalism itself, to which it added a new operater, *WITH*, hereby opening up for a new rule type that would allow a more efficient grammar writing by fusing entire rule blocks with shared contexts into one, integrated rule.

On behalf of the workshop organizers,

Trond Trosterud and Eckhard Bick

Organizing Committee

Workshop organizers

Eckhard Bick, Research lector, Institute of Language and Communication, University of Southern Denmark
Tino Didriksen, Developer, GrammarSoft ApS; University of Southern Denmark
Kristin Hagen, Senior engineer, Tekstlaboratoriet, University of Oslo
Kaili Müürisep, Senior research fellow, Institute of Computer Science, University of Tartu
Trond Trosterud, Professor in Sámi computational linguistics, University of Tromsø
Linda Wiechetek, Senior engineer, University of Tromsø

Program Committee / Reviewers

Eckhard Bick (Chair)
Edit Bugge
Lina Lejdebro Enwald
Kristin Hagen
Katri Hiovain-Asikainen
Kaili Müürisep
Anssi Yli-Jyrä
Flammie A. Pirinen
Jack Rueter
Daniel Glen Swanson
Trond Trosterud
Elaine Uí Dhonnchadha
Kevin Brubeck Unhammer
Linda Wiechetek

Table of Contents

Attribution of Quoted Speech in Portuguese Text

Eckhard Bick
University of Southern Denmark
eckhard.bick@gmail.com

Abstract

This paper describes and evaluates a rule-based system implementing a novel method for quote attribution in Portuguese text, working on top of a Constraint-Grammar parse. Both direct and indirect speech are covered, as well as certain other text-embedded quote sources. In a first step, the system performs quote segmentation and identifies speech verbs, taking into account the different styles used in literature and news text. Speakers are then identified using syntactically and semantically grounded Constraint-Grammar rules. We rely on relational links and stream variables to handle anaphorical mentions and to recover the names of implied or underspecified speakers. In an evaluation including both literature and news text, the system performed well on both the segmentation and attribution tasks, achieving F-scores of 98-99% for the former and 89-94% for the latter.

1 Introduction

In text linguistics, quote attribution is the task of identifying the person or entity behind a quoted utterance, as well as delimiting the quote itself. Automatic tools capable of robustly performing this twin task may be used in a variety of scenarios, such as the extraction of character networks from novels (e.g. Elson et al., 2010; Vala et al., 2016; Santos et al., 2022), voice assignment in text-to-speech systems, information extraction from news channels (Sarmento and Nunes, 2009) or the validation of social media claims (Janze and Risius, 2017). In this paper we will distinguish between speakers and sources, associating the former with direct quotes (1a) and the latter with indirect quotes (1b) and in-text source references (1c). Both speakers and sources may be either narrative characters (including a first-person narrator) or real-life people, organizations and institutions, depending on whether the text in question is fiction or non-fiction (e.g. news).

(1a) [“/--]The attack caused widespread fires[“], the mayor said.

(1b) The mayor also said that the attack caused widespread fires.

(1c) According to the mayor, Vitali Klitschko, the attack caused widespread fires.

Quote attribution must be distinguished from a wider approach to source identification that would include, for instance, photo or article sources (2a), or the bibliographic attribution of scientific findings (2b).

(2a) Russian reservists leaving for the front. EPA/YURI K.

(2b) Yearly precipitation increased by 24% over the decade (Moulder & Huggins, 2016)

The work presented here excludes these source types and focuses on quote attribution.

Though there is a growing body of research in the field, most work has been carried out for English. Among the (few) publications about our own target language, Portuguese, are (Mamede & Chaleira, 2004) and (Sarmento and Nunes, 2009), who address characters in children's' books and news quotes, respectively. Most systems use various machine-learning (ML) techniques exploiting, besides frequency and recency of mention, features from morphosyntactic and other available linguistic annotation, not least named entity recognition (NER). For instance, Elson and McKeown (2010) treat attribution as an ML classification task, while O’Keefe et al. (2012) use ML with a sequence-labelling method. Systems also differ in task scope. Thus, Ek et al. (2018) annotate addressees, including collective addressees, in

Proceedings of the NoDaLiDa 2023 Workshop on Constraint Grammar - Methods, Tools and Applications, pages 1–9

addition to speakers, which they categorize as either explicit, anaphoric or implied[1].

Our own work is different from most current research not only in terms of target language (Portuguese) and by including both literature and news data, but also because it pursues a rule-based approach, exploiting the Constraint Grammar paradigm (Bick and Didriksen 2015) to harness complex context conditions and assign relational tagging for coreference resolution and speaker mark-up. Apart from linguistic transparency and efficiency in a sparse-data situation, rule-based systems support straight forward genre adaptation, even in the complete absence of training data, by adding new rules (or exceptions to existing ones). Interestingly, O'Keefe et al. (2012) found that a simple rule-based baseline[2] outperformed their ML approach for speaker attribution in literature, and proved to be on par for for mixed news (Sidney Morning Herald). Only for the Wall Street Journal did ML work better.

The scope of our attribution annotator includes speakers/sources in both direct and indirect speech, regardless whether the information is explicit, anaphoric or implied. However, given the fact that accuracy for listener/addressee identification tends to be almost half that obtainable for speaker/source (Yeung and Lee, 2017; Ek et al. 2018), the former was not included here. Given that speaker attribution is a high-level linguistic task, we believe that the methodology of our Portuguese set-up can be generalized to other languages, or at least be used for inspiration and comparison.

2 Parsing technology

Our attribution rules are run on top of a full morphosyntactic and semantic annotation provided by the PALAVRAS parsers (Bick 2014). The system provides reliable tagging and disambiguation for lemma, POS, inflection, and semantic class including named entities, as well as dependency and frame structures. Our own rules are an extension of PALAVRAS' anaphora and coreference relations and make use of existing ID-links. While our rules make reference to many different tag types, the most important ones are, obviously, the speech- and speaker-related ones: +HUM semantic classes, speech verbs and their subjects and object clauses, as well as related semantic roles (§ATR – attribute, §ID – identity, §SP – speaker, §MES – message).

The attribution annotator does not use CG's traditional MAP, SELECT and REMOVE rules, as we do not treat attribution as a disambiguation task. Rather, tags are inserted using CG3's SUBSTITUTE rules type in a sequential fashion – supporting tags first (quote delimiters, quote heads and quoting verbs), then the primary tags (speaker/source), progressing from safe/close contexts to more heuristic long-distance contexts. In addition, we use the relatively new CG3 feature of stream variables[3] to store and retrieve text and paragraph-level information about turn-taking, previous speaker and speaker-associated noun phrases.

3 Quote and dialogue segmentation

3.1 Quote types and annotation

The density of quotes is extremely text-dependent. Thus, in their work on classical English literature, Elson and McKeown (2010) found a spread of 19-71% of text included in quotes. For our own, Portuguese data the quote density was also high, higher for news (51.7%) than for the literature sample (42.1%). Interestingly, there was a considerable difference when comparing direct with indirect quotes, with the former being frequent in literature (87.3% of all quotes), but rare in the news data (11.7% of all quotes) – a difference with a possible bearing on performance, as indirect quotes are more likely to have a close/syntactic link to a quoting verb, while direct speech may occur in isolation, with quoting information left implicit or provided in another sentence.

1 Some systems handle only the explicit category, and others who do include anaphoric pronouns and np's may do so verbatim without resolving the reference by linking to a name. Our own system handles all three types, but attempts to resolve all as names, with noun phrases as an under-specified fall-back solution.

2 search backwards from the end of the quoted sentence until the nearest speech verb, then pick the nearest named entity mention.

3 Stream variables are different from CG3's tag unification variables. While the latter are local and limited to the containing rule, stream variables are are part of the input/output stream and visible to all rules. Stream variables can be set either externally or by the CG rules themselves. In the newest edition of CG3, both names and values of stream variables can be written, matched and excerpted using regular expressions and ordinary tag variables.

In Portuguese, direct quotes may be optionally marked with either opening quotation marks (3c, 4b, common in news text) or a dash (3a-b, common in literature), both of which will be repeated if the quote continues after a "backward" quoting verb (3a). Opening quotation marks are always matched with closing quotation marks (3c), but closing dashes are only used before quoting verbs, not if the latter precedes the quote (3b). In the absence of other punctuation, a comma is added between a quote and a "backward" quoting verb. In one quoting style (3d), the closing comma is the only visible quote delimiter.

We use three quote delimiter tags: <quote-edge> (start), <quote-end> (stop) and <quote-ana> (for quote continuation after an inquit). In addition, the quoting verb is tagged <v-quote>. The quote itself is marked on its syntactic top node (3a-d), with <quote> for direct speech, or <quote-ind> for indirect speech.

(3a) -- <quote-edge> *É verdade, faz* <quote> *medo, mas é bonito* - <quote-end> *acrescentou* <v-quote> *Eulália.* - <quote-ana> *Hei* <quote> *de ir sempre ver.* [it's true, it is frightening, but it is beautiful, Eulália added. I have to watch it all the time]

(3b) *Era, pois, sincero, quando, de joelhos, exclamou* <v-quote>: – <quote-edge> *Porque te amo* <quote>. [He was, thus, sincere, when he, on his knees, called out: "Because I love you"]

(3c) " <quote-edge> *A situação na região de Odessa é muito difícil"* <quote-end>, *começou por dizer* <quote> *o Presidente ucraniano* [The situation in the region of Odessa is very difficult, the Ukrainian president said when he took the floor]

(3d) *Em Odesa, registaram-se* <quote> *ataques com "drones" durante a noite, que deixaram grande parte da região sem eletricidade,* <quote-end> disse <v-quote> o chefe do Governo local, Maxim Marchenko. [In Odessa, during the night, drone attacks were registered, which left a large part of the region without electricity, the local governor, Maxim Marchenko, said.]

Automatic quote annotation has to distinguish quote segmentation from other uses of quotation marks (e.g. titles, literatim-markers [4a] or special words [3c]) and dashes (e.g. parenthetical material), and it has to take into account "forward" quoting constructions with a colon, but potentially no other delimiter. Also, a quote may encompass more than one utterance, so possible quotation marks or hyphens may be outside the window of analysis.

(4a) *O Presidente ucraniano agradeceu a Washington pela "forte parceria" e descreveu a visita de Biden como "histórica, oportuna e corajosa".* [The Ucrainian president thanked Washington for its "strong partnership" and described the Biden visit as "historical, timely and courageous".]

Given the underlying dependency annotation, the <quote>/<quote-ind> tags are enough to extract the quote even without the use of delimiter tags. If present, quoting verbs are either forward-(colon-style) or backward-pointing, but unlike the <quote> marker, <v-quote> may also be absent or implied (4b).

(4b) *A avaliação é do Ministério da Defesa britânico: "A contínua priorização de infra-estrutura nacional crítica (...)"* [The evaluation is the British Ministry of Defense's: "The continued targeting of critical national infrastructure (...)]

All six types of quote markers double as CG rule barriers (or barrier exceptions), especially when searching across multiple sentence windows, telling the rule "cursor" when it leaves or enters a quote, whether a sentence is part of a multipart quote, or – in dialogue – if a quote is adjacent or isolated by narrative body text.

Below are two simplified examples of <v-quote> mapping rules[4], relying on a speech-verb frame tag (<fn:speak>) and the presence of either a <quote-end> token (first rule) or a post-positioned human subject (second rule):

```
SUBSTITUTE (V) (<v-quote> V)
  TARGET VFIN + @FV + <fn:speak>
  (*-1 <quote-end> BARRIER NON-KOMMA);

SUBSTITUTE (V) (<v-quote> V)
  TARGET VFIN + @FV + <fn:speak>
  (cr @<SUBJ + N-HUM-person);
```

4 In their simplified form, the rules could be combined by using the OR convention to include both context conditions in one rule: ((*-1 ....) OR (*1 ....))

While direct quotes have the syntactic structure of main clauses and may constitute independent sentences, indirect quotes have subclause structure and a dependency link to the quoting verb. In this case, we add <quote-ind> to the top node of the subclause[5], again facilitating dependency-based quote extraction (5a-b). Note that in Portuguese, indirect quotes may be infinitives (5b), a construction common in the news domain.

(5a) *Ela disse que não o queria* <quote-ind> *fazer.* [She said that she didn't want to do it.]

(5b) *Ele disse ser* <quote-ind> *absurda a alegação.* [He said that the allegation was absurd.]

The identification of speech verbs is of great importance for other annotation tasks. Thus, it triggers the recognition of a comma as <quote-end>, and a preceding clause as <quote>. Above all, however, speech verb identification facilitates speaker identification, either directly, through a proper noun subject dependent, or indirectly through reference links for zero-subjects and pronouns. Like Elson and McKeown (2010), we use an external semantic resource to identify speech verbs, but instead of their lexical WordNet categories, we use verb classes from PALAVRAS' framenet annotation (Bick 2022), which have the advantage of being disambiguated and linked to tokens carrying semantic role tags for speaker (§SP) and message (§MES), respectively. Verbs without a speech frame proper (e.g. *wonder,* attack) may still be identified if they are reinforced by a post-positioned +HUM subject in the pattern:

…, + finite_verb + human_subject

For continuation verbs (*continue, add, insist*) the subject is usually omitted in Portuguese (corresponding to pronoun use in English), but in sentence final position, the pattern is still a reliable speech indicator:

…, + continuation_verb [adverbials] .

3.2 Dialogue and turn-taking variables

In addition to quote annotation, dialogue segmentation has obvious benefits for speaker attribution (Yeung and Lee, 2017)[6]. For instance, a vocative mention in one quote paragraph may help identify the speaker of an immediately preceding or following quote paragraph. In our system, we set a turn-taking variable when a quote-opening token is found, alternating the variable value between 1 and 2 in order to keep track of speaker turns. The variable is un-set after the paragraph that contained the quote-opener. The turn-taking variable either directly as a CG3 local variable (LVAR) or as a tag mapped on relevant tokens. It allows us to unify speakers across alternating turns, propagating information from e.g. the first, explicitly quoted, turn to later turns[7] by the same speaker in the same dialogue chain. The rule example captures a speaker variable \(...\) from an established SPEAKER tag in the same turn type (here: turn 1) either left or right in the window span (*0W). To make sure the turns belong to the same dialogue span, there is a BARRIER for top node verbs (@FV) that are not quoted (<quote>) or quoting (<v-quote>), i.e. that represent ordinary, narrative text. The captured variable ($1) is then inserted as SPEAKER on the target quote.

```
(R-1) SUBSTITUTE
  (<quote>) (<quote> <SPEAKER:$1>v)
  TARGET (<quote> <turn-1>)
  (*0W (<SPEAKER:\(.*\)>r <turn-1>)
    BARRIER @FV - <quote> - <v-quote>) ;
```

4 Attribution methods

We assign a <SPEAKER:...> tag to each direct quote, and a <SOURCE:...> tag to each indirect quote, mapped on the <quote> and <quote-ind> tags, respectively. Ideally, the value for SPEAKER and SOURCE should be a name, but as a fall-back, definite noun phrases are accepted. With the exception of anonymous or group utterances, quotes in literature should ultimately be traceable to a character name, but

5 The semantic parser will already have marked the subclause as §MES (message), but on its main verb, which may be different from the top-node finite verb.

6 Naturally, this is relevant only if the work in question contains structured, but unexplicit dialogue. In their own experiment, Yeung and Lee (2017) did not find any improvement for the New Testament.

7 This kind of speaker propagation also works backward. To achieve this, we have to run the attribution grammar twice: Because CG works sequentially from left to right, "future" (later-in-text) information will only be accessible for reference in a repeat run of the grammar. A section rerun would have the same effect, but the cg3 formalism only foresees this for disambiguation grammars, not pure substitution or relation grammars.

in the news domain, sources may be institutions (e.g. the Ministry of Defense) or officials not linked to a human name, but to a function (e.g. the local mayor or a Red Cross representative). The rule examples and variable use discussed in this section focus on the <SPEAKER:...> tag, but mostly hold for the <SOURCE:..> tags as well.

4.1 Direct attribution: Quoting verbs and source references

The safest speaker identification is through an associated quoting verb (<v-quote>), found either (a) as a dependency head, (b) immediately after a <quote-end> tag or before a <quote-ana> tag, or (c) as the closest top-level verb before a quote-opening colon. Departing from the speech verb, the prioritized order of speaker extraction will then be the following:

1. subject dependent: name
2. subject dependent: noun phrase or pronoun with a <REF:....> name tag, or r:ref relation leading to a name
3. no surface subject, but a <REF:...> or <SUBJ:...> name tag, or a r:ref name relation, on the verb

For (b) and (c), in order to reach the relevant left or right quote delimiter and quoting verb, sentence boundaries may have to be crossed in the case of multi-sentence quotes. As mentioned in section 3, this can be made safer by using the various <...quote...> markers as barriers or barrier exceptions, but ultimately there is the risk of confusing a sentence boundary with a paragraph boundary and retrieving a wrong speaker value. We therefore introduced a paragraph-numbering variable that can be checked to see if the encountered <v-quote> and is located within the same paragraph. In dialogue, where each turn fills a whole paragraph, the turn-taking variable can be exploited to the same end.

Another scenario for direct attribution is the use of reference pointers in adverbial constructions with *segundo, conforme* and *de acordo com* (all meaning ‘according to’). Independent of word order and syntax, these proved to be very safe source indicators for citations[8] occurring in the same sentence. Rule R-2 looks left or right (*0) for the trigger words *segundo* or *conforme*, harvesting a referent name or lemma either directly form their argument (c=child) or from the +HUM subject in a dependent clause. Typically, PALAVRAS will have assigned these constructions a §META role.

```
(R-2) SUBSTITUTE
  (V) (VSTR:<SOURCE:$1> V)
  TARGET <fmc>
  (*0 ("segundo") OR ("conforme")
    LINK (0 §META LINK c @P<)
      OR (c §META)
      OR (1 VFIN LINK 0 <fn:speak>
        LINK cr N/PROP-HUM + @<SUBJ)
    LINK 0 (<REF:\(.*\)>r) OR ("<(.*)>"r)) ;
```

4.2 Indirect or implied attribution and speaker propagation

Similarly, if a quote has no associated quoting verb of its own, but the preceding sentence contains a direct or indirect quoting construction, its speaker may be copied ($2 variable below) as long as both sentences are in the same paragraph[9] (cf. the ‘par’ $1 variable in the rule below).

```
(R-3) SUBSTITUTE
  (<quote>) (<quote> <SPEAKER:$2>v)
  TARGET (<quote>)
  (0 (VAR:par=/\([0-9]+\)/r))
  (*-1 <quote-edge> OR <quote-ana>
     BARRIER <quote-end> OR <v-quote>
     LINK -1 >>> LINK *-1W ALL-ORD
     LINK *-1 <v-quote> BARRIER <quote>
     LINK cr @<SUBJ
     LINK *-1 (<SPEAKER:\(.*\)>r)
     LINK 0 (VSTR:LVAR:par=$1)) ;
```

If there is no speaker mention or speech verb subject reference found in the same paragraph, and not even an anonymous speaker can be assigned, the grammar defaults to speaker alteration using a pair of stream variables, speaker (R-5) and oldspeaker (R-4). When a new speaker is established, the speaker variable is reset and its previous value stored as “oldspeaker”. Unless a turn is marked as “continuing” (verb frame), it is “oldspeaker” that

---

8 It should be noted, though, that such citations, unless framed in quotation marks in their entirety, may be rephrasings or gists, and need not exhibit the same literatim fidelity as direct or indirect speech with a quote verb.

9 if not, they may belong to different turns, with different speakers.

will be used for hitherto unattributed quotes (R-6).

```
(R-4) SETVARIABLE (oldspeaker) (VSTR:$1)
  TARGET (<SPEAKER:.*>r)
  (0 (VAR:speaker=/\([^\\^].*\)/r)) ;
```

```
(R-5) SETVARIABLE (speaker) (VSTR:$1)
  TARGET (<SPEAKER:\([^\\^].+\)>r) ;
```

```
(R-6) SUBSTITUTE (<quote>)
  (<quote> VSTR:<SPEAKER:$1>)
  TARGET (<quote>)
  (0 (VAR:oldspeaker=/\(.*\)/r))
  (NEGATE *1W <v-quote>
    BARRIER @FV - <quote>
    LINK 0 <fn:continue> OR <fn:add>
  (NEGATE *0 @VOK
    LINK 0 ("$1"v) OR (<REF:$1>v)) ;
```

4.3 Reference links, tags and variables

An important aspect of our attribution method is keeping track of who is who through stream variables and through the use of co-reference links and tags. The task is a formidable one: 40-50% of quote chunks do not contain a quoting verb, leaving the speaker implied or obliquely mentioned. Of those that do feature a quoting verb, the latter may lack a surface subject (28% in our literature data, 14% in news), or the surface subject may be an anaphorical pronoun or underspecified noun phrase.

For anaphora resolution, we use CG3's ADDRELATIONS operator to establish referent links between pronouns and underspecified noun phrases and a target referent, optimally a named entity (NE). The equivalent solution for subject-less verbs are elliptic-subject relations. In both cases, name targets will also be mapped, as <REF:name> tags, on the anaphorical element itself. This is useful for "promoting" the antecedent information, if link targets are themselves anaphorical (e.g. chains of pronouns or subject-elliptical verbs), in which case the ultimate name referent may be outside the rolling CG focus window (set to ±6 sentences in this grammar). In (6), for instance, the second quoting verb, *disse* [said], is subject-elliptic, but the anaphora rules will link it to the nearest top-level human subject to the left, in this case the explicit subject (*Biden*) of the first quoting verb, *afirmou* [asserted]. To this end, contextual syntax- and semantics-informed rules are much safer than e.g. just going for the closest NE or even human NE, which in this case would yield the wrong speaker, *Zelensky.*

(6) *"A Ucrânia resiste. A democracia resiste", afirmou Biden, ao lado de Zelensky. "Putin achou que a Ucrânia era fraca e que o Ocidente estava dividido", disse.* ["Ukraine resists. Democracy resists", Biden asserted, with Zelensky by his side. "Putin thought Ukraine was weak and the West divided," he said.]

In addition to anaphora links, we use stream variables to store relevant established information across analysis windows. Apart from the afore-mentioned turn-taking and paragraph variables, we store "new speaker name" and "old speaker name" (cf. section 4.2). For anaphora resolution, we set a variable for most recent top-level subject and a "social function" variable (professions and functional titles) for nouns referring to names. This type of information storing goes beyond simple fixed variables, as it can't be known beforehand, which and how many social functions a text may contain.

Thus, every time a common-noun reference has been resolved to a proper noun (7a), the latter is stored as the value ($1 in R-7) of a *newly created* variable ($2 in R-7) carrying the name of the former, appended to a prefix *nattr-* (name attribute). The prefix allows a blanket resetting of all noun-speaker variables at major breaks in the text, such as chapter or news article headlines.

```
(R7) SETVARIABLE
  (VSTR:nattr-$2) (VSTR:$1)
  TARGET ("<(.+)>"r PROP £hum)
  + (<NA:Hprof/\(.*\)>r) ;
```

The name value can then be retrieved (as $2 in R-8) for "underspecified" speakers ($1 in R-8), i.e. speaker mentions that were nouns rather than names (7b), exploiting information from an earlier paragraph (7a) in the same article or chapter.

(7a) *Bombardeamentos (…). O anúncio foi feito pelo* ***governador*** *da região,* ***Pavlo Kyrylenko****, no Facebook: "(...)".* [Bombardments … The announcement was made by the region's governor, Pavlo Kyrylenko, in Facebook: ...]

(7b) *A cidade é (…). Segundo o* ***governador****, (…) , "é impossível determinar ..."* [The town is

… According to the governor, … "it is impossible to determine ..."]

(R-8) SUBSTITUTE

```
(<SPEAKER:.*>r) (VSTR:<SPEAKER:$2>)
TARGET (<SPEAKER:\([a-z].*\)>r)
(0 (VSTR:VAR:nattr-$1=/\(.*\)/r)) ;
```

As a fall-back alternative to variable-based name retrieval, a single-noun reference can be expanded through rules harvesting and adding its post-nominal dependents. This way, *governador* (governor) can be specified as *governador de Lugansk* (the Luhansk governor), and sources such as ministries and intelligence services may be specified for resort or nationality.

5 Evaluation

With two main applications in mind, character cast extraction and information extraction, the system was evaluated on two very diverse sets of data, historical literature to cover the former, and news text to cover the latter. Specifically, we used the first 7% of José do Patrocínio's "Os Retirantes", published in 1879 (13164 parser tokens, ca. 380 quotes), and a collection of articles[10] from the *Público* newspaper covering the Ukraine war between 3 August 2022 and 20 February 2023 (35076 parser tokens, ca. 610 quotes). In addition to extreme differences in vocabulary, syntax, style and orthography, there was a marked difference in quotation style, with 97.6% direct (SPEAKER) quotes in "Os Retirantes" and 63.9% indirect[11] (SOURCE) quotes in the war news. The relative number of quoted sentences was higher in the literature sample, but the quotes were longer in the news text.

5.1 Quote recognition and segmentation

Quote recognition worked well or both text types and both quotation styles (table 1), with F-scores of around 99% for direct speech (<quote>), and 97%[12] for indirect speech (<quote-ind>). The good results for quote recognition are not surprising given that most quotes in the literature sample were in separate paragraphs and marked with an opening dash, while the prevailing indirect quotes in the news sample were dependency-linked to a speech verb.

mark-up	**literature**			**news**		
	R	**P**	**F**	**R**	**P**	**F**
quote	98.1	99.7	98.9	99.1	98.7	98.9
v-quote	100	98.9	99.4	100	97.8	98.9
quote-edge	100	98.1	99.0	100	98.6	99.3
quote-end	97.6	97.6	97.6	98.6	100	99.3
quote-ana	96.1	96.1	96.1	100	100	100
quote-ind	(100)	(100)	(100)	96.1	98.4	97.2

Table 1: Precision, recall and F1-score for quote recognition and segmentation

Annotation of the quoting verbs (<v-quote>) and segmentation markers (<quote-edge>, <quote-ana> and <quote-end>) for direct speech was also very robust, but a little less so for the (sometimes ambiguous) dashes used in literature for <quote-end> and <quote-ana> than for the quotation marks used in news. For indirect quotes, segmentation was implicit and hence unevaluated, with the quoting verb assumed to be the dependency head of the <quote-ind> node, and segmentation implied by the dependency structure.

5.2 Speaker/source attribution

The second part of the evaluation concerned the more difficult task of speaker and source attribution. Most existing research has focused on the former rather than the latter. For English, in a cross-author testing, Ek et al. (2018) achieved F-scores of 41.3-73.4 (mostly around 70). Elson & McKeown (2010) achieved a higher F-Score (83%), for a mixed-author quote corpus, but included the gold-annotation of the preceding quote as a feature for their classifier. He et al. (2013) report 74.8-82.5 for speaker identification in direct quotes, with a ±1-paragraph window. As expected, explicit speakers were unproblematic (F=100), while anaphoric and implied speakers were harder, with F-scores of 76.4 and 63.1, respectively.

Our own system for Portuguese achieved an F-score of 94.7% for speaker identification in

10 https://www.publico.pt/2022/02/24/infografia/russia-invade-ucrania-guia-visual-entender-guerra-661 [retrieved 23 February 2023]

11 While direct quotes are clearly marked as such, the borderline for indirect quotes is a little more fuzzy, and based on verb semantics. For instance, the object clauses in the frames *defend cognitively* and *reject* were not counted as quote, while those in *promise* frames were included.

12 There were too few instances (9) of indirect speech in "Os Retirantes" to meaningfully compute performance.

news, and 92.0% for literature, with relatively small differences between recall and precision (table 2). One obvious explanations for the difference between literature and news is that we counted (full definite) noun phrases as correct speaker references, but not pronouns, and that the former are more typical of news text than in literature, where there is a limited, but more constant, set of characters with anaphorical or implied references to names. For both text types, results are about one percentage point better if computed for correctly identified quotes only. For the news domain, accepting underspecified noun phrases as speaker also led to higher scores (F=96.1). Source identification (indirect speech and "according to"-type references) proved to be more difficult than direct quote attribution[13], with 50% higher error rates (F=91.4 for news[14]).

mark-up	literature			news		
	R	P	F	R	P	F
SPEAKER	91.3	92.8	**92.0**	94.9	94.5	**94.7**
on corr. quotes	92.8	93.0	92.9	95.8	95.8	95.8
w/ underspecif.	-	-	-	96.3	95.9	96.1
SOURCE	88.9	88.9	**88.9**	90.4	92.5	**91.4**
w/ undersp.	-	-	-	94.3	96.5	95.4

Table 2: Precision, recall and F1-score for speaker and source

These results, albeit measured with a "soft", inspection-based method without a pre-determined gold-standard annotation[15], compare favourably with prior research for English, where good results may depend on the exclusion of anaphora and implied mentions, e.g. (Zhang and Liu, 2022) with an F-score of 87% for explicit speakers in direct speech. The best and most comparable results for Portuguese were reported by Sarmento and Nunes (2009), who crawled direct and indirect news quotes, but pursued an extreme precision-oriented approach, achieving P=98.2% for speaker attribution by excluding all anaphorical references and accepting only explicit named-entity mentions as speaker candidates.

Error inspection revealed that about 1/3 of attribution errors in the news data could be traced back to parsing errors, mostly syntactic function / dependency errors, but also a couple of POS errors (both leading to false positives). For the literature sample, due to the prevalence of direct quotes and scarcity of syntactically linked surface speaker names, errors were mostly due to complex rule interaction problems rather than (local) base parse errors[16].

6 Conclusion

We have shown how a rule-based and context-aware (CG) system can reliably exploit existing dependency and framenet annotation for quote attribution in Portuguese, stressing the importance of long-distance referent links and the use of annotation-aware speaker and turn-taking variables.

Given that the context conditions in the attribution rules make use of higher-level, universal linguistic categories and relations rather than language-specific vocabulary or morphology, it appears likely that the rules could be ported to other languages with similar base parser support.

It is an added advantage of the approach that the same set of rules appears to work for both news and literature. For the news domain, with real-life information extraction in mind, future versions could exploit external resources to link NE mentions to unique identifiers and to resolve definite noun phrase mentions that are not clear from immediate context, e.g. for politicians and officials referenced with their function rather than their name.

13 However, the portion of errors related to 'according-to' constructions, were due to an easy-to-fix rule bug, corrected post-evaluation. Thus, the under-performance for SOURCE attribution is now likely smaller than reported.

14 The same holds for literature, but given the few instances of SOURCE in our sample, this should be reevaluated on a different novel, with more indirect speech.

15 Gold annotations are typically piece and parcel of ML methodology, because they are used for training, too. For a rule-based approach, gold data would be evaluation-only, and hence relatively more expensive. It would also counteract the fast improvements and genre adaptation typical of rule-based development, because changes in e.g. category inventory or tokenization will make the (fixed) gold data difficult to use.

16 One specific problem was that quotes were sentence-split from a following quoting verb if the quote ended in a question or exclamation mark, as the latter were treated as window delimiters by the CG. This was fixed by disambiguating between "breaking" and "non-breaking" question and exclamation marks.

References

Eckhard Bick. 2014. PALAVRAS, a Constraint Grammar-based Parsing System for Portuguese. In: Tony Berber Sardinha & Thelma de Lurdes São Bento Ferreira (eds.), *Working with Portuguese Corpora*, pp 279-302. London/New York:Bloomsburry Academic.

Eckhard Bick and Tino Didriksen. 2015. CG-3 - Beyond Classical Constraint Grammar. In: Beáta Megyesi: *Proceedings of NODALIDA 2015, May 11-13, 2015, Vilnius, Lithuania*. pp. 31-39. Linköping: LiU Electronic Press.

Eckhard Bick. 2022. PFN-PT: A Framenet Annotator for Portuguese. In Heliana Mello & Fernanda Farinelli (eds.), *The computational treatment of Brazilian Portuguese*. Domínios de Linguagem. [S. l.], v. 16, n. 4, pp. 1401-1435.

Adam Ek, Mats Wirén, Robert Östling, Kristina N. Björkenstam, Gintarė Grigonytė & Sofia Gustafson Capková. Identifying Speakers and Addressees in Dialogues Extracted from Literary Fiction. In *Proceedings of LREC 2018*. ELRA. pp- 817-824

David K. Elson, Nicholas Dames, and Kathleen McKeown. 2010. Extracting social networks from literary fiction. In *Proceedings of the 48th Annual Meeting of the Association for Computational Linguistics*, pages 138–147, Uppsala, Sweden. ACL.

David K. Elson and Kathleen McKeown. 2010. Automatic Attribution of Quoted Speech in Literary Narrative. In *Proceedings of the AAAI Conference on Artificial Intelligence*, 24(1),. pp. 1013-1019. https://doi.org/10.1609/aaai.v24i1.7720

Hua He, Denilson Barbosa and Grzegorz Kondrak. 2013. Identification of Speakers in Novels. In *Proceedings of the 51st Annual Meeting of the Association for Computational Linguistics (Volume 1: Long Papers).* pp. 1312-1320.

Christian Janze and Marten Risius. 2017. Automatic Detection of Fake News on Social Media Platforms. In *Proceedings of the 21st Pacific Asia Conference on Information Systems (PACIS).*

Tim O'Keefe, Silvia Pareti, James R. Curran, Irena Koprinska, and Matthew Honnibal. 2012. A Sequence Labelling Approach to Quote Attribution. In *Proceedings of EMNLP 2012.* ACL. pp- 790-799

Nuno Mamede and Pedro Chaleira. 2004. Character identification in children stories. In *Advances in natural language processing*, pp. 82–90. Springer.

Diana Santos, Roberto Willrich, Marcia Langfeldt, Ricardo Gaiotto de Moraes, Cristina Mota, Emanoel Pires and Rebeca Schumacher. 2022. Identifying literary characters in Portuguese: Challenges of an international shared task. In Vládia Pinheiro et al. (eds.) *Proceedings of PROPOR 2022* (Fortaleza, Brazil). pp. 413-419. Springer

Luis Sarmento and Sergio Nunes. 2009. Automatic extraction of quotes and topics from news feeds. In *DSIE'09 - 4th Doctoral Symposium on Informatics Engineering* (Porto, Portugal, 5-6 February 2009).

Hardik Vala, Stefan Dimitrov, Davud Jurgens, Andrew Piper, and Derek Ruths. (2016). Annotating characters in literary corpora: A scheme, the Charles tool, and an annotated novel. In Nicoletta Calzolari et al. (eds), *Proceedings of LREC 2016*. ELRA → extraction of character networks

Chak Yan Yeung and John Lee. (2017). Identifying speakers and listeners of quoted speech in literary works. In *Proceedings of the Eighth International Joint Conference on Natural Language Processing* (Volume 2: Short Papers). pp. 325–329. Asian Federation of Natural Language

Yuanchi Zhang and Yang Liu. 2022. DirectQuote: A Dataset for Direct Quotation Extraction and Attribution in News Articles. *Proceedings of the 13th Conference on Language Resources and Evaluation (LREC 2022)*, pp. 6959–6966. ELRA

WITH Context: Adding Rule-Grouping to VISL CG-3

Daniel Swanson
Department of Linguistics
Indiana University
dangswan@iu.edu

Tino Didriksen
Institute of Language
and Communication
University of Southern Denmark
tinod@sdu.dk

Francis Tyers
Department of Linguistics
Indiana University
ftyers@iu.edu

Abstract

This paper presents an extension to the VISL CG-3 compiler and processor which enables complex contexts to be shared between rules. This sharing substantially improves the readability and maintainability of sets of rules performing multi-step operations.

1 Introduction

When writing constraint grammars for more complex tasks, such as parsing or translation, situations often arise in which a particular context triggers multiple operations. For example, when writing a dependency parser, the head of a word and its grammatical function label are often determined jointly. Similarly, for tasks such as translation that involve modifying either the syntactic structure or the linear order of the words, a change in one word will typically necessitate changes to its dependents as well.

One way to handle such cases in CG is to have each operation repeat the entire set of contextual tests, which is tedious to write, difficult to read, and error-prone to maintain. Another way is to add an initial rule which checks the conditions and adds a label to the target word and then have each other rule simply check for the appropriate label. This, however, leads to a proliferation of single-use tags in the grammar (which may need to be documented), and does not solve the problem that rules which operate on relationships between words, such as `SETPARENT` or `ADDRELATION` still need to duplicate contextual tests in order to locate the second cohort.

To address these difficulties, we extend the VISL CG-3 processor (Bick and Didriksen, 2015) with the operator `WITH`, which matches a context and then runs multiple rules, all with that same context. This new operator has been released as part of VISL CG-3 version 1.4.0. Section 2 describes the syntax of this operator, Section 3 provides examples of its application in various domains, Section 4 discusses its performance implications, and Section 5 concludes.

2 Syntax

An example of the `WITH` operator in use is given in (1).

(1)

```
WITH (n) IF (-1* (det)) {
  SETCHILD (*) TO (jC1 (*)) ;
  SETCHILD REPEAT (*) TO
    (-1*A (adj) LINK -1* _C1_) ;
} ;
```

Here the context being matched is a noun preceded at any distance by a determiner. The subsequent rules are then run with the noun as their target, so the target can be the any set (if a rule specifies a target set, then it will only be run if that set matches the target of the `WITH`). The rules can refer to the cohorts matched by the contextual tests of the `WITH` using either the position specifiers `jC1`, `jC2`, ... `jC9` for the first through ninth tests, respectively, or using the magic sets `_C1_`, `_C2_`, ... `_C9_`.

Thus the first `SETCHILD` attaches the determiner (here matched with `jC1 (*)`) to the noun and the second one finds any adjectives which are between the noun and the determiner (here matched with `-1* _C1_`) and attaches them to the noun. By default, rules inside a `WITH` are run once when the `WITH`, but `REPEAT` has the usual effect of causing the rule to be repeated until it has no effect.

As this example and those in the next section show, the `WITH` operator, while not strictly increasing the expressivity of CG, does allow many

Proceedings of the NoDaLiDa 2023 Workshop on Constraint Grammar - Methods, Tools and Applications, pages 10–14
May 22, 2023 ©2023 Association for Computational Linguistics

sets of rules to be written in a much more readable and maintainable manner.

3 Examples

The following subsections give examples of applications of `WITH` to particular domains.

3.1 Dependency Parsing

A set of rules for dealing with numbers and determiners found in the parser from Swanson and Tyers (2022) is presented in Figure 1.

3.2 Translation

Multi-step transformations are also relevant in machine translation. For instance, transforming the dependency tree in (2) for the Hebrew phrase ראש השנה to the appropriate tree for the English "the head (or beginning) of the year", given in (3).

(2)

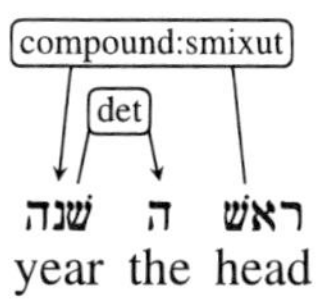

(3)

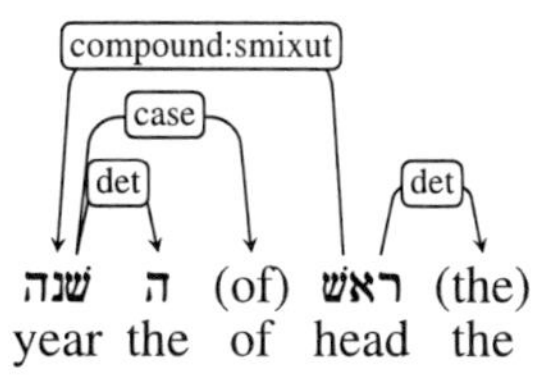

This can be accomplished using the rules in (4).

(4)

```
WITH (n @compound:smixut)
  IF (p (n))
  (NEGATE c (@compound:smixut))
{
  ADDCOHORT
    ("<the>" "the" det def @det)
    BEFORE (*)
    IF (c (@det)) (jC1A (*)) ;
  ADDCOHORT
    ("<of>" "of" pr @case)
    BEFORE WITHCHILD (*) (*) ;
  UNMAP (@compound:smixut) (*) ;
  MAP (@nmod) (*) ;
} ;
```

Note, particularly, the `UNMAP` followed by the `MAP`, which would otherwise be extremely difficult to do correctly, since the `MAP` would otherwise need some way of finding the cohort it was supposed to replace the tag of, when that cohort no longer has that tag.

3.3 Morphological Disambiguation

Even in tasks that typically do not require composite operations, such as disambiguation, there is often a high degree of duplication in contextual tests which can benefit from the use of `WITH`. For example, in the Apertium morphological disambiguator for Norwegian Nynorsk (Unhammer and Trosterud, 2009) 1504 (38.5%) of the 3903 rules have at least 2 tests and share at least 90% of those tests with another rule in the file. The rules in (5) are given as an example of such overlap.

(5)

```
SELECT:4144 (adj pl) IF
    (NOT 0 fv)
    (NOT 0 subst)
    (NOT 0 det)
    (1 komma/konj)
    (-1C fl-det)
    (NOT 1 subst/adj)
    (NOT 2 adj)
;
SELECT:4145 (adj pl) IF
    (NOT 0 fv)
    (NOT 0 subst)
    (NOT 0 det)
    (NOT 0 pos)
    (-1C fl-det)
    (NOT 1 subst/adj)
;
```

The duplicate tests can be extracted, as in (6).

(6)

```
WITH (adj pl) IF
    (NOT 0 fv)
    (NOT 0 subst)
    (NOT 0 det)
    (-1C fl-det)
    (NOT 1 subst/adj)
{
    SELECT (adj pl) IF
        (1 komma/konj)
        (NOT 2 adj) ;
```

```
# Original rules

MAP @flat BigNumber + Number IF (-1 Number) ;
SETPARENT @flat + Number (NOT p (*)) TO (-1 Number) ;

MAP @conj Number
    IF (-1 @cc LINK -1* Number BARRIER (*) - @flat) ;
SETPARENT @cc (NOT p (*)) TO (1 Number + @conj) ;
SETPARENT Number + @conj (NOT p (*))
    TO (-1* Number - @flat BARRIER (*) - @cc - @flat) ;
REMCOHORT IGNORED WITHCHILD (*)
    Number + @conj OR Number + @flat
    IF (p Number) ;


# Rules rewritten using WITH

WITH BigNumber + Number (-1 Number) (NOT p (*)) {
  MAP @flat (*) ;
  SETPARENT (*) TO (jC1 (*)) ;
  REMCOHORT IGNORED (*) ;
} ;

WITH Number (-1 @cc) (-2 Number) (NOT p (*)) {
  MAP @conj (*) ;
  SETCHILD (*) TO (jC1 (*)) ;
  SETPARENT (*) TO (jC2 (*)) ;
  REMCOHORT IGNORED WITHCHILD (*) (*) ;
} ;
```

Figure 1: A set of rules for parsing Hebrew number phrases according to Universal Dependencies (Nivre et al., 2020), with and without the `WITH` operator. The original set of rules is taken from the parser described in Swanson and Tyers (2022). In each set, the first group of rules matches a phrase such as שלוש מאה "three hundreds" and makes the second word dependent on the first with the label `flat`. Then the second group matches a phrase like תשע וערבע "nine and four" and attaches the conjunction to the second number and the second number to the first, giving the second number the label `conj`. Finally the dependent words are ignored (treated as deleted for the remainder of parsing, but included in the output).

Grammar	Rules	`WITH` Groups	Runtime	Cohorts	Cohorts/s	Speedup
Hebrew Original	346	0	5.58 s	65K	11,756	0%
Hebrew safe-setparent	346	0	4.80 s	65K	13,690	14%
Hebrew WITH	349	9	4.93 s	65K	13,310	12%
Norwegian Original	3903	0	142.26 s	174K	1,225	0%
Norwegian WITH	3903	180	79.43 s	174K	2,194	44%

Table 1: Performance comparison of the rewrite of the Ancient Hebrew dependency parser from Swanson and Tyers (2022) and an automated refactoring of the Norwegian Nynorsk morphological disambiguator from Unhammer and Trosterud (2009). "Hebrew Original" is the parser presented in the first paper, "Hebrew safe-setparent" is the same parser, but with `safe-setparent` flag enabled, and "Hebrew WITH" is a version that has been partially refactored to use `WITH` groups and also slightly expanded. The parser using `WITH` also uses `safe-setparent`. "Norwegian Original" is the disambiguation grammar distributed by Apertium as of April 2023 and "Norwegian WITH" is an automated transformation of that grammar. In neither language is the grammar using `WITH` perfectly identical to the original in terms of output.

```
    SELECT (adj pl) IF
        (NOT 0 pos) ;
} ;
```

Here the 5 contexts that are shared between the two rules are written only once and each rule need only specify the part that differs, substantially clarifying the purpose of having distinct rules in this instance.

4 Performance

The performance impact of adding a `WITH` group to a grammar is generally small, though measurable. In this section we present the effects on two grammars: the Ancient Hebrew dependency parser from Swanson and Tyers (2022) and the Apertium Norwegian Nynorsk morphological disambiguator (Unhammer and Trosterud, 2009). The results are listed in Table 1.

When `WITH` improves performance, it is generally due to a reduction in the number of contextual tests that need to be evaluated. However, the deduplication of tests is balanced by the fact that `WITH` must evaluate them sequentially in order to populate the `_Cn_` magic sets whereas for most rules the VISL CG-3 processor will internally update the order so as to start with the test that is most likely to fail.

Thus, when refactoring a complex grammar by hand where the total number of `WITH` groups added is likely to be small, the potential speedup is relatively small and is easily overwhelmed by the impact of new rules. In the Hebrew parser, for example, the effect of rearranging the contextual tests of roughly 30 rules (9% of the grammar) into 9 `WITH` groups was negated by adding half a dozen new ones (overall a 2% slowdown), and both of these effects are minor compared to the effect of an unrelated change that removed one test from each of 135 rules (a 14% speedup).

On the other hand, in the Norwegian grammar, the relationships between rules are generally quite simple and we were thus able to write a script that automatically merged adjacent rules which shared the same target and had at least 5 contextual tests in common into a `WITH` group. The results of this conversion are not perfect (just over 5% of the 10K sentences in our test data have different output), but they are good enough for an approximate comparison. The script grouped 1636 rules (42% of the grammar) into 180 `WITH` groups, increasing the speed of the disambiguator by 44%.

5 Conclusion

In this paper we have presented the `WITH` operator, an extension of VISL CG-3 to allow collections of rules to be grouped into composite operations. As shown in the examples, this addition is likely to be useful to grammar authors approaching a wide variety of tasks and can even have a significant impact on grammar performance if deployed on a large scale.

References

Eckhard Bick and Tino Didriksen. 2015. Cg-3—beyond classical constraint grammar. In *Proceedings of the 20th Nordic Conference of Computational Linguistics (NODALIDA 2015)*, pages 31–39.

Joakim Nivre, Marie-Catherine de Marneffe, Filip Ginter, Jan Hajič, Christopher D. Manning, Sampo Pyysalo, Sebastian Schuster, Francis Tyers, and Daniel Zeman. 2020. Universal Dependencies v2: An evergrowing multilingual treebank collection. In *Proceedings of the Twelfth Language Resources and Evaluation Conference*, pages 4034–4043, Marseille, France. European Language Resources Association.

Daniel Swanson and Francis Tyers. 2022. A Universal Dependencies treebank of Ancient Hebrew. In *Proceedings of the Thirteenth Language Resources and Evaluation Conference*, pages 2353–2361, Marseille, France. European Language Resources Association.

Kevin Unhammer and Trond Trosterud. 2009. Reuse of free resources in machine translation between nynorsk and bokmål. In *Proceedings of the First International Workshop on Free/Open-Source Rule-Based Machine Translation*, pages 35–42.

To ð or not to ð
A Faroese CG-based grammar checker targeting ð errors

Trond Trosterud
UiT The Arctic University of Norway
trond.trosterud@uit.no

Abstract

Many errors in Faroese writing are linked to the letter *ð*, a letter which has no corresponding phoneme, and is always omitted intervocally and wordfinally after a vowel. It plays an important role in the written language, disambiguating homophone but not homograph forms like infinitive *kasta* 'throw' from its participle *kastað*. Since adding a hypercorrect *ð* or erroneously omitting it often results in an existing word, these errors cannot be captured by ordinary spellcheckers. The article presents a grammar checker targeting *ð* errors, and discusses challenges related to false alarms.

1 Introduction

The article addresses a central problem in written Faroese: How to correct errors arising from erroneously writing or omitting the letter *ð* in such a way that the resulting errouneous form is an existing word. A typical case of *ð* omission is (1), and an instance of superfluous *ð* is (2)[1].

(1) Tey hava serliga ***tosa** um at í
they have especially talk.V.Inf about that in
Grønlandi er tað grønlendskt sum skal vera
Greenland is it Greenlandic that shall be
fyrsta mál.
first language
'In particular, they have talked about the fact that in Greenland Greenlandic shall be official language'

(2) Eg ***haldið** at orsøkin til at HB
I consider.V.Imp.Pl that reason for that HB
vann móti KÍ var ein einastandandi
won against KÍ was a unique
liðinnsatsur.
team.effort
'In my opinion, the reason why HB won against KÍ was an outstanding effort by the team'

In (1), *ð* is omitted from the correct supine form *tosað*, resulting in an infinitive, and in (2) the correct present first person singular form *haldi* has received a hypercorrect *ð*, resulting in a plural imperative form.

The challenge is to correct such errors. The approach presented here is to build a grammar checker on top of a grammatical analysis of Faroese, where the erroneous patterns are identified and the correct forms are presented to the user, accompanied by an explanation. The grammar checker is already part of the web-based version of the Faroese spell checker[2], and the main challenge at the present stage is thus to have a good precision. Testing the recall of the grammar checker is obviously relevant for a thorough evaluation, but this falls outside the scope of the present article.

The article is structured as follows. First, section 2 shortly presents relevant aspects of Faroese and of the morphological and grammatical components providing the input to the grammar checker. Section 3 presents the grammar checker. Section 4 presents the evaluation material and discusses the results. Finally comes a conclusion.

2 Background

2.1 Faroese grammar and the letter *ð*

Faroese is a North Germanic language spoken by appr. 80.000 people, mainly on the Faroe Islands. The grammatical structure of written Faroese contains the traditional three gender (masculine, feminine, neuter) and four case (nominative, accusative, genitive, dative) system and person inflection for verbs known from Old Norse and Ice-

[1] In the examples, the wordform flagged as an error will be given in **bold**. When the wordform is wrong, it is marked with an asterisk. When it is correct, and the alarm is false, there is no asterisk.

[2] https://divvun.no/korrektur/gramcheck.html

Proceedings of the NoDaLiDa 2023 Workshop on Constraint Grammar - Methods, Tools and Applications, pages 15–19
May 22, 2023

landic. Contrary to these languages, person inflection in Faroese is found only in the singular. For a presentation, see (Thráinsson et al., 2012).

Faroese orthography is conservative and the written standard differs considerably from the spoken language, which itself is divided in several dialects. Relevant to the present discussion is the letter *ð*, which plays a central role in the inflectional system of the written language. The *ð* may be added to both nominal stems, giving definite forms, and verbal stems, giving participles or imperative plural forms. As shown by (Thráinsson et al., 2012) p. 20, "the letter *ð* [does] not as a rule have any phonetic value intervocalically or word-finally after a vowel". Word form pairs distinguished by the *-ð* suffix thus give rise to homonymy pairs in speech, but not in writing. Central homonymy cases are shown in table 1[3].

MS cat.	Form	MS cat.	Form
V.Inf & Prs.Pl.	kalla	Ptc. & Sup.	kallað
V.Prs.Sg1 & N.Dat.Indef.	fari	Ptc & Sup N.Nom.Def N.Acc.Def	farið
V.Inf & A.Def	norska	Ptc. & Sup.	norskað

Table 1: Systematic homonymies. Example words: *kalla* V 'call, name', *fara* V 'leave, travel', *far* N 'track', *norsk* A 'Norwegian', *norska* V 'make Norwegian'.

2.2 Faroese morphology and disambiguation

The Faroese morphology is handled by a finite state transducer (Beesley and Karttunen, 2003), described in (Trosterud, 2009). The morphological description was mainly based upon (Thráinsson et al., 2004), but in order to get a comprehensive description of the morphology, the transducer was built with the inflection classes from (Poulsen et al., 1998). The lexicon was based upon (Poulsen et al., 1998), but complemented with frequent words from the online Faroese corpus[4]. Issues not covered by these sources were addressed in cooperation with Heðin Jákupsson.

Faroese inflectional morphology is rich in homonymy, with on average 4.0 analyses per word form. In order to disambiguate this, the grammar checker uses a disambiguator based upon constraint grammar (Karlsson, 1990). The constraint grammar is presented in (Trosterud, 2009).

3 The Faroese grammar checker

3.1 Technical background

The system is built on a pipeline of modules as presented in Wiechetek (2019). The pipeline uses the free open source implementation HFST (Lindén et al., 2013) for finite-state automata and VISLCG-3 (Didriksen, 2016) for constraint grammar. Both are included in the *GiellaLT* infrastructure (cf. Moshagen et. al., (2013) for a presentation).

The grammar checker uses the finite state transducer presented in 2.2, but instead of the ordinary disambiguator it uses a relaxed version of it. The reason for this is that the disambiguator presented in 2.2 is based upon the assumption that the input is correct. Since this assumption does not hold for a grammar checker, certain disambiguation rules had to be relaxed in order not to remove relevant target forms.

The Faroese grammar checker is part of a multilingual infrastructure *GiellaLT*, which includes language models either released or on a functional (beta) level for appr. 40 languages. The source code is publicly available[5].

The Faroese grammar checker is already available for use in the Divvun grammar checker interface [6]. Given that the grammar checker is still in an early stage, its main purpose is to make the Faroese spell checker (which is integrated in the grammar checker) available also on Google docs and on MS Word for Macintosh, platforms who do not allow third-party spell checkers. For the present stage of the grammar checker development it is thus more important to avoid false alarms than to achieve a good coverage.

3.2 Errors to be targeted

In this article, only a part of the grammar checker rule set is presented, the one relevant to a certain type of *ð* errors, errors due to spoken language homonymy due to *ð* suffixes in one of the forms. The errors targeted are the confusion of supine (= neuter participle when combined with an auxiliary) and infinitive forms, the confusion of participle

[3]Abbreviations: Prs = present tense, Ptc = participle, Sup = supine, Indef/Def = (in)definite

[4]`https://gtweb.uit.no/f_korp`

[5]The source code for Faroese is found here: `https://github.com/giellalt/lang-fao`.

[6]The Divvun grammar checker interface makes it possible to use the grammar checker together with MS Word and Google docs, cf. `https://divvun.no/en/korrektur/gramcheck.html`

and first person singular forms, as well as the confusion of supine and present plural forms.

4 Evaluation

4.1 The material

As evaluation corpus was used a subset of the Faroese BLARK text corpus (Simonsen et al., 2022). It contained 9.0 million words, from the following genres (table 2):

Genre	Words
Students 17-20 years	77.674
Magazines	339.751
Blogs	285.637
Online news	7.180.722
Newspapers	1.138.988
Total	9.022.772

Table 2: Text genres in the test corpus

The largest category is online news, containing texts both from the Faroese Broadcasting company KVF and the online news portal website *Portalurin*. The magazines included are *MEGD* and *Starvsbladid*. More details are given in the metadata of the BLARK itself.

4.2 Results and analysis

The corpus was run through the grammar checker[7], and each alarm (reported error) was manualy evaluated. Looking at the results by genre, we get the results shown in table 3. For each genre, the table gives the number of alarms (cases the grammar checker flags as erroneous) as well as whether they actually are wrong (TP, or true positive) or not (FP, or false positive). Precision is calculated as the number of true positives divided by all alarms.

Genre	**Alrms**	**Alrms /100k**	**TP**	**FP**	**Prec. (%)**
17-20yrs	9	11.6	7	2	77.8
Mags	30	8.8	23	7	76.7
Blogs	20	7.0	11	9	55.0
Onl.nws	370	5.2	274	96	64.7
Newsp.	2	0.2	2	0	100.0
Total	431	4.8	317	114	73.5

Table 3: Evaluation

[7]The grammar checker used for testing was the version from Nov 4th 2022, github.com/giellalt/lang-fao/blob/main/tools/grammarcheckers/grammarchecker.cg3

For all genres the percentage of alarms was low, around or below ten per 100.000 words. As can be seen, the errors are somewhat more common for genres where we would expect less proofreading. Investigating recall is outside the scope of the present paper, but it seems likely that only a part of the real amount of (relevant) errors has been found. Precision, or the percentage of correct alarms, varies from genre to genre, with 73.5 % calculated on the corpus as a whole.

Looking now at the alarms according to grammatical type, we get a different picture, with more variation in the precision. Table 4 gives an overview. The rule types are written on the format *wrong form* $\rightarrow$ *correct form*.

Rule	**Total**	**TP**	**FP**	**Prec.**
sup $\rightarrow$ inf	44	37	7	84.1 %
inf $\rightarrow$ sup	287	230	57	80.1 %
prfptc $\rightarrow$ sg1	8	6	2	75.0 %
sup $\rightarrow$ sg1	56	30	28	53.6 %
sup $\rightarrow$ prspl	36	14	23	38.9 %
Total	431	317	117	73.5 %

Table 4: Alarms according to rule type

The most common error type was infinitive for supine, the type shown in (1). It contained 66.5 % of all the alarms in the evaluation material. The error type also had a good precision rate, 80.1 %.

The false alarms typically involved errors in part of speech disambiguation. A case in point is the false alarm shown in (3).

(3) Eg havi **illgruna** um
I have.V.Prs.Sg1 suspicion.N.Sg.Acc about
at tað er tí mótargument
that.Sbj that.Det is because counter.argument
mangla, ella hvussu?
is.missing, or what?
'My suspicion is that this is because the counter arguments are missing, don't you agree?'

The form *illgruna* is also a verb, with a participle *illgrunað*. The grammar checker has thus erroneously identified it as an infinitive-for-supine pattern. The quite frequent form *illgruna* occurred in several false alarms, and should be identified as part of the collocation *hava illgruna um* 'be suspicious about'.

Another false alarm, this case one of accidental and not systematic homonymy, is (4).

(4) Hava vit ikki **egna**
have.V.Prs.Pl we not own.A.Sg.Acc.Indef
søgu, mál og identitet?
history, language and identity
'Don't we have our own history, language and identity'

Here, the accusative form of the common adjective *egin* 'own' is accidently identical to the verb *egna* 'to bait, to add fishbait on the hook'. In a revised version this should be solved by including *egna* in a set of infinitives not to be corrected. Almost all false alarms for this rule were of these two types.

The inverse error type, supine for (correct) infinitive, shown in (5), was more rare, with 10 % of the alarms. This type showed the best precision of all the error types.

(5) Ja hvat annað skal man ***tosað** um?
Yes what else shall one talk.V.Sup about?
'Well, what else should one have talked about?'

For this rule type, some of the false alarms were due to the pronoun *man* 'one', that (probably for puristic reasons) was not included in the Faroese dictionary (Poulsen et al., 1998) and therefore also not in the language model, and thus was confused for the homonymous present singular form of the modal *munna* 'may'. An example of this type is (6).

(6) Tað sær út til, at øll hesi árini
that looks out to, that all these years
hevur man ikki **megnað** at fáa
have.V.Prs.Sg3 one not achieve.V.Sup to get
broytingar í tær samsýningar, sum eru, sigur
changes in the fees, that are, says
løgmaður
lawyer
'It looks like one during all these years has not been able to get any changes in the existing fees, the lawyer says.'

The two next error types represent hypercorrect use of *ð* in first person singular form, as in example (2) above. Another example is (7).

(7) Eg ***sitið** eitt mjørkatungt
I sit.V.Sup one dark.heavy
summarkvøld í einum hugnaligum
summer.evening in one cosy
køki í Havn
kitchen in Tórshavn
'A dark summer evening I sit in a cosy kitchen in Torshavn'

For this error type, the precision was lower than for the supine/infinitive ones. The main problem for these rules was that they failed to capture a first person verb *havi* 'have.V.Prs.Sg1' to the left (8).

(8) Mangan havi eg **sitið** og verið
Often have I sit.V.Sup and been
ónøgd við, at meira ikki hevur verið
dissatisfied with, at more not has been
gjørt til tess at vinna okkum betri sømdir
done in.order.to get us better regard
'Many a time I have been dissatisfied by the fact that not more has been done in order to achieve a better reputation'

The problem was the preceeding disambiguation rule, which errouneously removed the verb reading of *havi* due to a typo in the tag for first person pronouns. *havi* was then analysed as a noun, and the grammar checker thus flagged *sitið* as an error.

A further weakness of the grammar checker revealed during evaluation was that it flagged Sg1 errors also when the target form did not end in *-ið*.

(9) Í mong harrans ár havi eg **skrivað** til
in many Lord's years have I write.V.Sup to
damubløðini tey kalla, men altíð
women's.magazines they say, but always
undir dulnevni.
under pseudonym
'For God knows how many years I have written to the so-called women's magazines, but always under pseudonym'

The point here is that *skrivað* is not a likely misspelling of first person *skrivi*, contrary to *sitið/siti*. The rule should thus have been restricted to the inflection classes with supine forms in *-ið*.

When it finds a potential error, the grammar checker suggests a form to replace it, whenever possible. In some cases the error identification was correct whereas the suggestion was not. One example is the supine form of *vera* 'to be', which is *verið*. This form occurred in several correctly flagged Sup $\rightarrow$ Sg1 errors, e.g. (10). .

(10) Eg ***verið** fullkomiliga
I be.V.Sup completely
fríkendur
aquit.V.PrfPtc.Msc.Sg.Nom.Indef
'I was completely acquitted'

Since the rules assume that the confused forms are supine and first person singular, it suggested the form *eri*, the first person present of *vera*. The form *verið*, however, is not a likely confusion of *eri*. It turned out that the target form here was not the copula, but the verb *verða* 'to become', which first person form is *verði*. Since the *ð* is not pronounced in this phonological context, the form is a homonym of *verið*. What is called for is thus a separate rule for this important verb, suggesting *verði* whenever *verið* occurs in first person singular contexts.

5 Conclusion

This article has presented an early version of a Faroese grammar checker, targeting errors related to inflectional forms containing the suffix *ð*. Even though the grammar checker still contains some obvious errors, the precision is quite good, over 80 % for the most frequent *ð* error type. With these errors corrected as well as an improved suggestion component, the present grammar checker may be seen as both a welcome addition to the Faroese spell checker as well as a pedagogical tool for pupils during the learning process.

The next steps for the grammar checker are to investigate the recall of the error types it already covers (to look at the *ð* errors the grammar checker fails to capture), and to include more error types. This is left for future research.

Acknowledgments

Thanks to my Faroese colleagues at Setur for inspiring discussions, to Heðin Jákupsson for cooperation on improving the morphological model, to Hanna Jensen for help with some tricky sentences in the evaluation dataset as well as for an analysis of the *verið* cases, and to the anonymous reviewers for useful comments.

References

Kenneth R. Beesley and Lauri Karttunen. 2003. *Finite State Morphology*. Studies in Computational Linguistics. CSLI Publications, Stanford, California.

Tino Didriksen. 2016. *Constraint Grammar Manual: 3rd version of the CG formalism variant*. GrammarSoft ApS, Denmark.

Fred Karlsson. 1990. Constraint grammar as a framework for parsing running text. In *COLING '90 Proceedings of the 13th conference on Computational linguistics*, volume 3, pages 168–173, Helsinki.

Krister Lindén, Erik Axelson, Senka Drobac, Sam Hardwick, Miikka Silfverberg, and Tommi A. Pirinen. 2013. Using HFST for creating computational linguistic applications. In Adam Przepiórkowski, Maciej Piasecki, Krzysztof Jassem, and Piotr Fuglewicz, editors, *Computational Linguistics: Applications*, pages 3–25. Springer Berlin Heidelberg, Berlin, Heidelberg.

Sjur N. Moshagen, Tommi Pirinen, and Trond Trosterud. 2013. Building an open-source development infrastructure for language technology projects. In *Proceedings of the 19th Nordic Conference of Computational Linguistics (NODALIDA 2013); May 22–24; 2013; Oslo University; Norway*, number 16 in NEALT Proceedings Series, pages 343–352. Linköping University Electronic Press.

Jóhan Hendrik W. Poulsen, Marjun Simonsen, Jógvan í Lon Jacobsen, Anfinnur Johansen, and Zacharis Svabo Hansen. 1998. *Føroysk orðabók*, volume 1-2. Føroya Fróðskaparfelag, Tórshavn.

Annika Simonsen, Sandra Saxov Lamhauge, Iben Nyholm Debess, and Peter Juel Henrichsen. 2022. Creating a basic language resource kit for Faroese. In *Proceedings of the Thirteenth Language Resources and Evaluation Conference*, pages 4637–4643, Marseille, France. European Language Resources Association.

Höskuldur Thráinsson, Hjalmar P. Petersen, Jógvan í Lon Jacobsen, and Zacharis Svabo Hansen. 2004. *Faroese: An overview and reference grammar*. Føroya Fróðskaparfelag, Tórshavn.

Höskuldur Thráinsson, Hjalmar P. Petersen, Jógvan í Lon Jacobsen, and Zacharis Svabo Hansen. 2012. *Faroese: An overview and reference grammar*. Føroya Fróðskaparfelag, Tórshavn.

Trond Trosterud. 2009. A constraint grammar for Faroese. In *Proceedings of the 17th Nordic Conference of Computational Linguistics. NEALT Proceedings Series*, volume 4, pages 1–7.

Linda Wiechetek, Sjur Moshagen, Børre Gaup, and Thomas Omma. 2019. Many shades of grammar checking – Launching a Constraint Grammar tool for North Sámi. In *Proceedings of the NoDaLiDa 2019 Workshop on Constraint Grammar: Methods, Tools and Applications, Turku, Finland*, volume 33 of *NEALT Proceedings Series*, Linköping, Sweden. Linköping University Electronic Press.

Towards automatic essay scoring of Basque language texts from a rule-based approach based on curriculum-aware systems

Jose Mari Arriola
HiTZ Center. Ixa Group
Basque Language and Communication
UPV/EHU
josemaria.arriola@ehu.eus

Jon Alkorta
HiTZ Center. Ixa Group
Basque Language and Communication
UPV/EHU
jon.alkorta@ehu.eus

Ekain Arrieta
HiTZ Center, Ixa Group
Languages and Information Systems
UPV/EHU
ekain.arrieta@ehu.eus

Mikel Iruskieta
HiTZ Center, Ixa Group
Languages and Literature Didactics
UPV/EHU
mikel.iruskieta@ehu.eus

Abstract

Although the Basque Education Law mentions that students must finish secondary compulsory education at B2 Basque level and their undergraduate studies at the C1 level, there are no objective tests or tools that can discriminate between these levels. This work presents the first rule-based method to grade written Basque learner texts. We adapt the adult Basque learner curriculum based on the CEFR to create a rule-based grammar for Basque. This paper summarises the results obtained in different classification tasks by combining information formalised through CG3 and different machine learning algorithms used in text classification. Besides, we perform a manual evaluation of the grammar. Finally, we discuss the informativeness of these rules and some ways to further improve assisted text grading and combine rule-based approaches with other approaches based on readability and complexity measures.

1 Introduction

Text classification of writing and reading materials is laborious and sometimes hard to do manually. Teachers that do not have a linguistic background do not feel confident in this task, but in some languages, researchers can use automatic text classification tools to point to some objective measures (Type Token Ratio, POS-based measures...). However, this automatic task is difficult to address for low resourced-languages. The classification of essays is worthy of interest because even if Basque Education Law mentions that students must finish compulsory secondary education at the CEFR B2 level and their undergraduate studies at the C1 level, there are no objective tests or tools that can discriminate between these levels. Using deep learning-based methods could be difficult for teachers as these do not follow the language curriculum or the learning stage of the student. If automated systems could describe the curriculum or the learning stage of the student in a way that the teachers can understand or employ, this would be very useful, and teachers would have an additional source of information where they could offer more adapted materials and teaching.

This work aims to explore rule-based models to classify written learner texts. The motivation of this work is to lighten the burden on teachers in the correction task. We want to contribute to the area of tools or applications to carry out objective tests automatically to fundamentally discriminate between levels B2 and C1. In this line, previous work (Zupanc and Bosnic, 2016) emphasises the role of automatic systems to help teachers:

> Automated essay evaluation represents a practical solution to a time-consuming, labour-intensive and expensive activity of manual grading of student's essays.

Furthermore, this approach could help to define language-based classification criteria that follow HEOC, the adult Basque learner curriculum (HABE, 2015).

One of the difficulties of classifying and grading essays is represented by the perceived subjectivity of the grading process. This issue may be

Proceedings of the NoDaLiDa 2023 Workshop on Constraint Grammar - Methods, Tools and Applications, pages 20–28
May 22, 2023

faced through the adoption of automated assessment tools for essays (Valenti et al., 2003).

There have been other studies of automatic classification for the Basque language but from different approaches (Castro-Castro et al., 2008; Zipitria et al., 2010, 2011; Azpillaga, 2022; Arrieta et al., 2023). We expand on these works and study how automatic text classifiers can benefit from Basque curricular grammar, a formalisation of the linguistic expressions described in the Basque curriculum.

Other similar works include a system for the Arabian language (Alqahtani and Alsaif, 2019) as well as feature-based machine learning approaches for Estonian (Vajjala and Loo, 2014) and monolingual, cross-lingual, and multilingual classification with three languages: German, Czech and Italian (Volodina et al., 2016). For Estonian, the best model reported by Vajjala and Loo (2014) reaches a prediction accuracy of 79%.

Regarding the automated essay-scoring task, Lim et al. (2021) conducted an automatic assessment using Automatic Essay Scoring systems. Gaillat et al. (2022), in their work, showed that early approaches were rule-based, but later systems relied on probabilistic models based on Natural Language Processing methods that exploit the corpus of learners. Their method exploits machine learning algorithms to classify learner writings with many metrics, including specifically-designed microsystem metrics. Microsystems are composed of several competing constructions (for instance the use of the article) grouped according to functional proximity. They can be defined as families of competing constructions in a unique paradigm. Results on internal data show that different microsystems help to classify essays from B1 to C2 levels (82% accuracy).

We follow a language- and curriculum-based approach: we formalise the expressions and linguistic phenomena described in the HEOC using CG3 (Bick and Didriksen, 2015), creating a level-informed grammar for Basque. The Basque CG3 Grammar contains 296 ADD rules that add language-level information. These rules are based on the linguistic indicators described for each level in the HEOC. We apply this grammar to the HABE-IXA Basque learner corpus (Arrieta et al., 2023), annotating the phenomena described by the curriculum. We use the information provided by the grammar to classify texts in binary and multi-class experiments and analyse which rules are relevant to discriminate different CEFR levels.

The paper is organised as follows: in Section 1, some background information on the Basque curriculum and text classification task is provided. Then our method to support essay classifying is described in Section 2. In this work, we evaluate and compare the results obtained using the CG3 grammar features with different algorithms. Detailed figures shall be shown in Section 3. After that, in the discussion, we propose some future lines of work, in Section 4. Finally, in Section 5 we sum up the main conclusions.

2 Method

We adapted the adult Basque learner curriculum based on the CEFR to create a rule-based grammar for Basque. First, we identified and defined phenomena and linguistic structures collected in HEOC that will be formalised for each level. The result of this task is what we call *Basque CG3 Grammar*.

The employed corpus contains essays written in official HABE (Basque Government Department for language certification) exams. It contains 480 texts (146,465 tokens) from the B1, B2, C1 and C2 CEFR levels. The corpus is balanced, it contains 120 essays of each level. These essays have been evaluated by at least two language expert testers. Following HABE's evaluation criteria, some of the texts have not obtained a passing grade for the exam, others have passed by a small margin and others have passed with good grades (see Table 1). It is available with CC BY-NC 4.0 license at: `https://doi.org/10.23728/b2share.81433fddcd06405f8505c7606b29ff99`

Lev.	Texts	Pass	Pass+	No pass	Tokens
B1	120	40	40	20	2,157
B2	120	40	40	20	28,319
C1	120	40	40	20	40,305
C2	120	30	17	73	56,271
All	480	150	137	133	146,465

Table 1: HABE-IXA corpus statistics (Arrieta et al., 2023)

To perform our curriculum-based classification approach, we have used the open-source grammar formalism VISL CG3 (Didriksen, 2003) which is compatible with other JAVA build systems such as CTAP (Chen and Meurers, 2016) by means of

Apache UIMA. This grammar was built by two expert linguists in CG3. The grammar contains 296 rules from A1 to C2 CEFR level, based on the HEOC (see Figure 1). These rules allow us to incorporate different types of linguistic information covering HEOC´s textual and language expressions as indicators of the development of linguistic competence and the development of the strategic competence that correspond to each level. After identifying these expressions, we annotate them with a custom tag corresponding to that rule. For example, for level C1 the following rule pays attention to the syntactic structures of completive sentences in which the subordinating particle (*ezen* stands for 'that') and the relation morpheme *-ela* appear, and adds the "C1_COMPLETIVES" tag:

ADD: C1_MAILAKO_MENDEKOAK (%C1_COMPLETIVES)

TARGET (KONPL)

IF (0 ADT OR ADL) (*-1 ("ezen"));

We apply our grammar in the morphologically annotated HABE-IXA corpus. Then, the results are filtered by removing linguistic instances that are either too common (the absolutive case, common nouns) or appear scarcely in this corpus (less than 10 total tags). The number of times each rule has been applied can be seen in Figure 1. It must be mentioned that the length of the essays in the corpus depends on its CEFR level, with B1 texts being the shortest and C2 the longest.

To evaluate this set of rules we have followed an intrinsic manual evaluation method checking whether the labels were applied correctly and an extrinsic automatic evaluation method where we use the annotation data to automatically classify texts depending on their CEFR level. For the latter, we want to see if the expressions identified by the CG3 rules encode relevant information about a text's level and complexity. We will perform the tasks of classification in two experiments:

- Binary classification (B2 or C1 level) using all rules and using the 10 most relevant rules.
- Multiclass classification (B1, B2, C1 or C2 level) using all rules and using the 10 most relevant rules.

3 Results

We evaluate the results through a detailed analysis consisting of an intrinsic and extrinsic evaluation.

	B1	B2	C1	C2	All
Total	198	284	259	148	889
Correct	188	273	247	120	828
%	94.94	96.13	95.37	81.08	93.14

Table 2: Results of the manual evaluation: precision of the Basque CG3 grammar.

Regarding the intrinsic manual evaluation method, we check manually if the labelled features were properly annotated using CG3 rules. The results in Table 2 show that in B1, B2 and C2 the precision is higher than 90%, and only C2 is below with 81.08% of accuracy.

During this evaluation, we realise that some rules are too general, so they are not informative, such as the use of common nouns, the use of absolutive case, the use of certain verbs tenses, and so on. Therefore, certain linguistic features of the HEOC are common at all levels and are very basic features that will have a greater presence in the texts, but from a qualitative point of view, they do not represent linguistic structures that help to determine a specific level. These common features will therefore be discarded in a future version because we will obtain this data by other means, for example using the Basque version of CTAP.

Regarding the extrinsic evaluation method, we proposed a classification task using only the CG3 rules: we use the data generated by our rule set to classify essays into a CEFR level. We want to see i) if the curriculum indicators that we have formalised as a ruleset allow us to determine the CEFR of an essay, and ii) which rules are most relevant for this classification.

We encode each text of the HABE-IXA corpus as a feature vector containing the extracted data of each rule as shown in Figure 2. We eliminate redundant information by filtering all the rule results that have a Pearson correlation higher than 0.95. Then, to avoid classification based on text length, we normalise each feature vector with the number of tokens in the text. Finally, we rescale the features to the same range (from 0 to 1) using a min-max scaler.

We split our data into training and evaluation sets (see Table 3), and we maintain this corpus split for all the experiments. For these classifica-

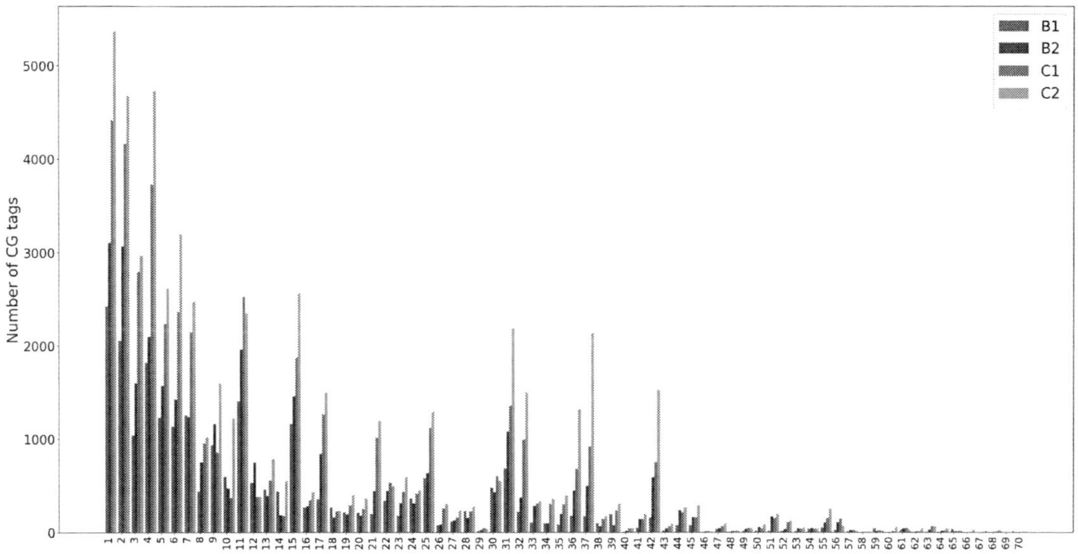

Figure 1: Each type of rule applied in the HABE-IXA corpus. Expressions in each of the levels of the corpus: B1, B2, C1 and C2. The complete list of rules is in the supplementary material.

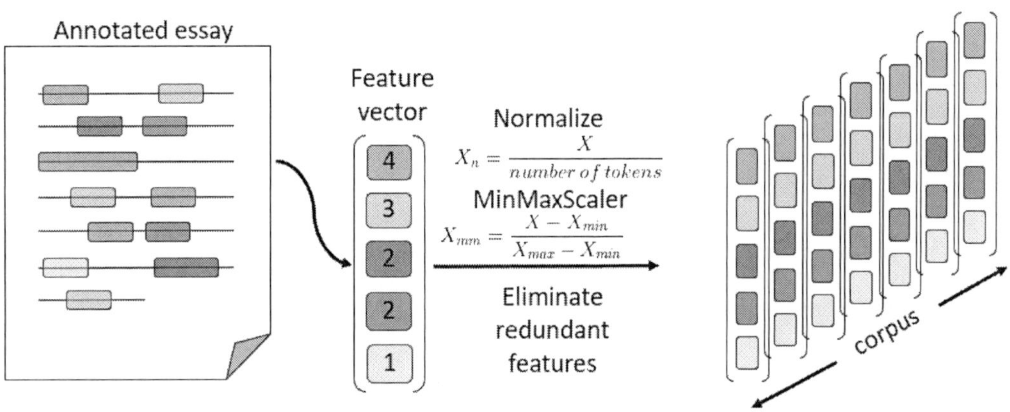

Figure 2: Preprocessing of the annotated texts and the feature vectors.

tion experiments, we use essays from the HABE-IXA corpus that passed their corresponding exam.

Classification	Train	Eval
Binary (B2-C1)	154	46
Multiclass	251	92

Table 3: Number of texts in training and evaluation sets.

To do so, we used Scikit-learn (Pedregosa et al., 2011) to train different types of machine learning models: i) support vector machine (SVM, RBF kernel and C = 1), ii) logistic regression classifier(LR), iii) random forest classifier (RF) (100 estimators, depth = 8) and iv) Naive Bayes classifier (NB). The results of these models are shown in Table 4.

	Binary			Multiclass		
	Train	Eval	Diff	Train	Eval	Diff
SVM	0.98	0.84	-0.14	0.97	**0.84**	-0.13
LR	0.95	0.76	-0.19	0.92	0.79	-0.13
RF	1.0	**0.87**	-0.13	1.0	0.80	-0.20
NB	0.85	0.82	-0.03	0.84	0.72	-0.12

Table 4: Evaluation set results of the CEFR level classifications, both binary (B1-C2) and multiclass (B1-B2-C1-C2), using all rules with different ML models.

As we can see in Table 4, the best results on the

evaluation data were obtained by the RF in the binary task and SVM in the multiclass task. The RF seems to overfit on train data in both tasks, so parameter optimization should be done in future work to avoid memorization issues. Naive Bayes classifiers obtain lower results, but training and evaluation accuracy are similar, suggesting that this could be a model that generalises better than the others.

We grouped the CG3 rules into four categories and analysed the importance of these categories in the classification task. We used permutation feature importance (Altmann et al., 2010) to measure the contribution of each of the features to the score of the classifier. The PFI permutates one feature at a time and measures the drop in accuracy of the model. The higher the loss of accuracy, the more important this feature was for the model. We measured the importance of the rules in the multiclass classification task using SVM, which obtained the best results. We show these results in Figures 3 and 4.

We see that rules "genitive case" and "indirect/reported question" are the most relevant rules for declension[1] and syntax, respectively. In Figure 4, we show the results for different groups of rules sorted according to the curriculum from A1 indicators to higher-level C2 indicators.

We show that we have rules for each level grouped in Verb, Declension and Syntax for levels A1, A2, B1, B2 and C1, and rules for Discourse phenomena in levels C1 and C2. Note that for C2 we do not have rules in other categories, since the curriculum only describes discursive features at this level. As we can see in Figure 4, Declension is the category that helps the most in the classification task for A1, A2, B2 and C1, but there is a large variance from one rule to another. The 10 most important features for the multiclass task (SVM) are shown in Table 5.

Finally, we show in Table 6 the results of the best models using only annotations from the 10 most important rules obtained with the PFI method. From the 4 models (RF, SVM, NL and NB), we only retrained the models that had the best performance using the entire grammar (RF and SVM).

Table 6 shows some rules are enough to have a strong classifier, which means that almost 10 rules do more than 90% of the classification task (91.95% of binary classification and 94.05% of multiclass classification task). But these 10 features do not seem that they are not as informative as the multidimensional phenomenon (lexis, grammar, discourse, morphology...) in which language is acquired or developed, because these 10 features are those to describe basic language forms from A1 to B2, but we don't find any feature from C1 (such as discourse markers, some type of subordinate clauses, subjunctive verbs...). Most of the distinctive features of these 10 basic features pertain to the field of morphology: case markers such as possessive/spatiotemporal genitive and ergative; the use of some kind of POS, for instance, nouns, pronouns, adverbs, verbal nouns and indeterminate modifiers; and the use of perfective verb aspect. The remaining feature corresponds to the syntax: the use of indirect/reported questions.

[1]Declension is not appropriate to describe Basque language, which is an agglutinative language. We use this terminology here because we try to reflect the linguistic information collected in the HEOC.

Rule	PFI
A2. Possessive genitive declension	0.073
A2. Spatiotemporal genitive	0.048
B1. Subordination. Indirect/reported question	0.047
B2. Adverbs	0.046
A1. Ergative declension	0.045
B1. Indeterminate	0.043
A2. Syntax. Perfective aspect	0.043
B2. Pronouns	0.038
B1. Verbal noun	0.035
B2. Nouns	0.030

Table 5: The rules and permutation feature importances for the most relevant features for the SVM classifier in the multiclass task.

	All rules	10 Rules
Binary - RF	**0.87**	0.80
Multiclass - SVM	**0.84**	0.79

Table 6: The classifier results using the entire ruleset and only the 10 most relevant rules.

4 Discussion

In this section, we explain some issues that may help to better understand the results: the size of the corpus and the application/design of the CG3 rules.

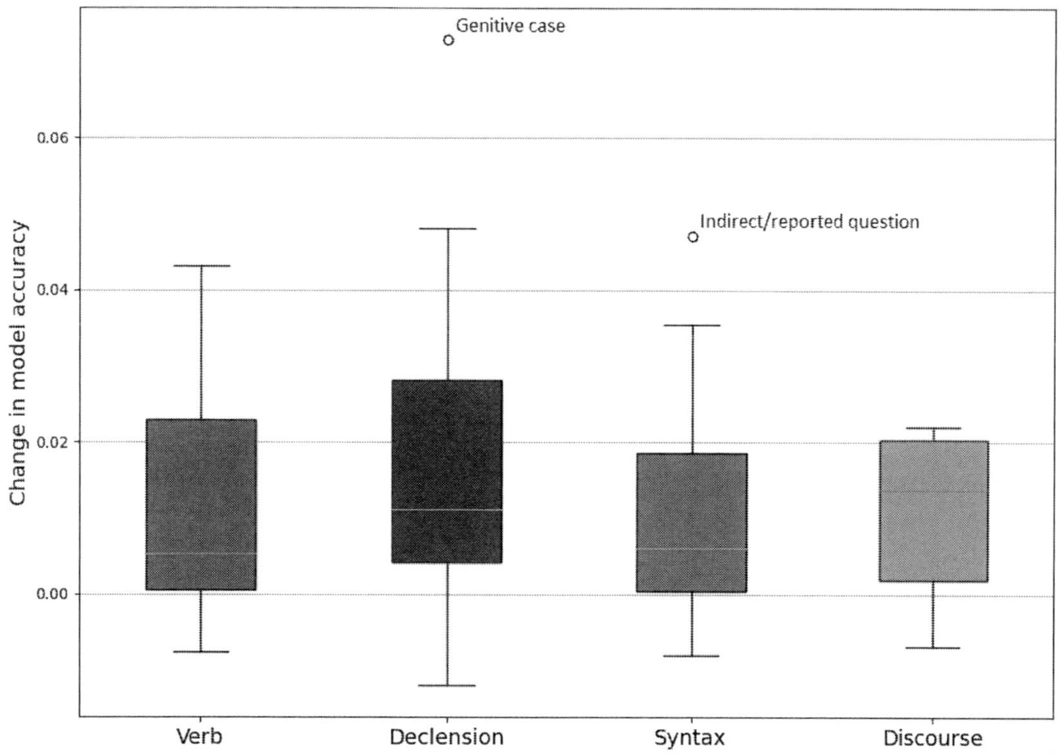

Figure 3: Permutation feature importance, measured as the change in the model's accuracy, for the different types of rules of the Basque CG3 Grammar. The outliers here represent the most relevant rule for each group.

The size of our corpus is one of the characteristics to take into account. The corpus is made up of 480 texts, 120 texts for each level (from B1 to C2). In total, there are 146,465 tokens in the corpus.

Compared to corpora with similar characteristics, our corpus is a bit smaller.

For example, Thewissen (2013) uses 223 texts with 150,000 tokens to study the evolution of errors through the different levels. Chen and Baker (2016) study lexical bundles in learner essays. The corpus used for that reason is bigger: it is made up of 585 essays and 202,154 tokens.

On the other hand, Lahuerta (2018) examines the texts of 100 Spanish EFL learners. The total number of tokens is 31,900. The corpus is used to study the accuracy and grammatical complexity. Yannakoudakis et al. (2018) want to predict proficiency levels in learner writing. To do this, they use two datasets: *i*) the learner output corpus (320 texts and 140,949 tokens) and *ii*) the expert input corpus (818 texts and 289,312 tokens).

As it has been observed, the size of our corpus is small compared to other similar works. Consequently, we have been able to find fewer errors, and this limits the accuracy of the results.

Apart from the size of the corpus, we think that it should be noted that the labels introduced by the rules indicate the level at which a given linguistic structure corresponds, this does not imply that they are only applied in texts corresponding to that level. For example, the labels of the most basic levels (A1, A2), such as common nouns, declension, verb tense and so on, also apply in texts of higher levels such as B2, C1, Basque C2... We can say that the grammar is coherent with the HEOC curriculum on which it is based. That means that each level meets all the features and linguistic phenomena of the levels below it.

Finally, from the grammarian perspective, the typology of these rules is varied (general phenomena and rules for specific constructions or words) and there have also been small differences in the way the labels are designed (for instance, for connectors we have general rule vs fine-grained rules). Therefore, it would be convenient to unify the criteria for creating rules for the next version.

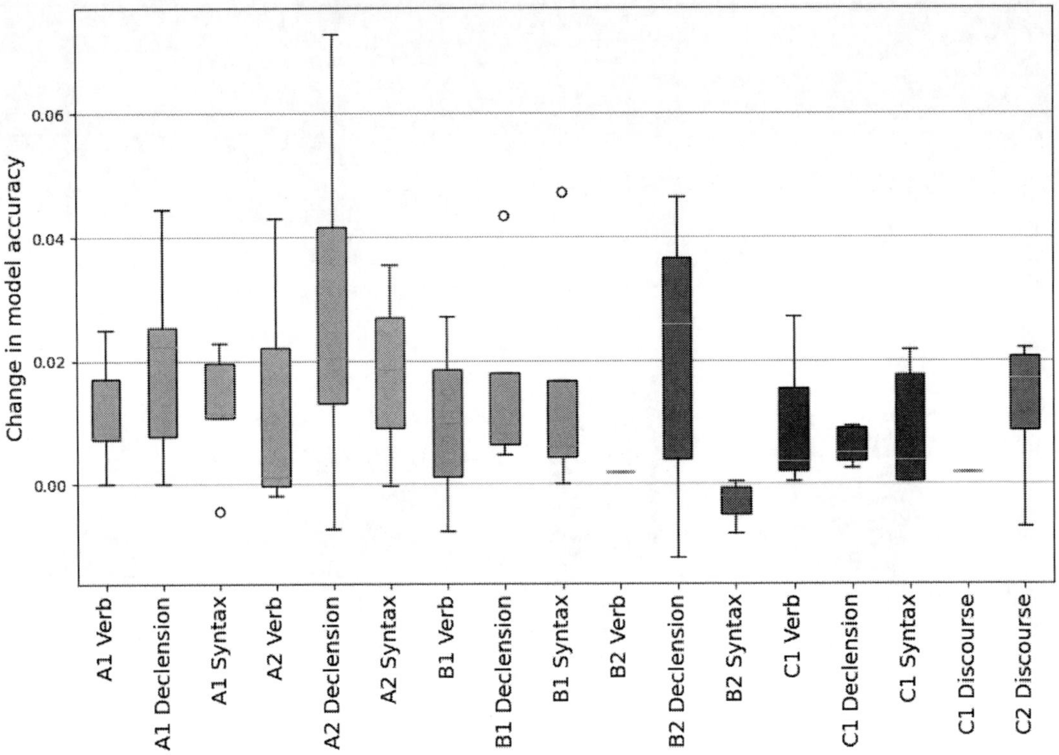

Figure 4: Permutation feature importance, measured as the change in the model's accuracy, for different groups of rules in the Basque CG3 Grammar, sorted according to the HEOC from A1 indicators to higher level C2 indicators.

5 Conclusion and future work

In this paper, we present the first CG3 version of the Basque grammar based on HEOC to grade written Basque students. The classification tasks performed on the experiments based on this first version show that the information provided by our rules is useful for discriminating different CEFR levels. There is a correlation between the greater the number of labels of different types, the higher the level of the text.

Our experimental results suggest that our approach has promising results, advancing the construction of automatic tools to test and discriminate between B2 and C1.

A more detailed analysis of the results shows also that the informativeness of these rules should be improved in the future. In that sense, we think that a redefinition of the principles for writing grammar benefits the explainability of the linguistic information added by the rules.

Finally, we believe that we will improve in assisted text grading by combining rule-based approaches with other approaches based on readability and complexity measures.

Acknowledgments

This work has been supported by the Basque Government: *Grupo Consolidado Ixa Taldea* (IT1570-22). We also acknowledge the funding from the Cost Action (CA19102) Language In The Human-Machine Era (LITHME).

References

Abeer Alqahtani and Amal Alsaif. 2019. Automatic evaluation for arabic essays: a rule-based system. In *2019 IEEE International Symposium on Signal Processing and Information Technology (ISSPIT)*, pages 1–7. IEEE.

André Altmann, Laura Toloşi, Oliver Sander, and Thomas Lengauer. 2010. Permutation importance: a corrected feature importance measure. *Bioinformatics*, 26(10):1340–1347.

Ekain Arrieta, Igor Odriozola, Xabier Arregi, and Mikel Iruskieta. 2023. Habe-ixa euskarazko idazmen-proben corpuseko idazlanen mailakatze automatikoa. *eHizpide*, 40(101).

Xabier Azpillaga. 2022. Euskarazko testuen komunikagaitasun-maila automatikoki sailkatzeko lehendabiziko urratsak. *Hizpide: helduen euskalduntzearen aldizkaria*, 40(99):3.

Eckhard Bick and Tino Didriksen. 2015. Cg-3—beyond classical constraint grammar. In *Proceedings of the 20th Nordic Conference of Computational Linguistics (NODALIDA 2015)*, pages 31–39.

Daniel Castro-Castro, Rocío Lannes-Losada, Montse Maritxalar, Ianire Niebla, Celia Pérez-Marqués, Nancy C Álamo-Suárez, and Aurora Pons-Porrata. 2008. A multilingual application for automated essay scoring. In *Advances in Artificial Intelligence–IBERAMIA 2008: 11th Ibero-American Conference on AI, Lisbon, Portugal, October 14-17, 2008. Proceedings 11*, pages 243–251. Springer.

Xiaobin Chen and Detmar Meurers. 2016. Ctap: A web-based tool supporting automatic complexity analysis. In *Proceedings of the Workshop on Computational Linguistics for Linguistic Complexity*, pages 113–119. The International Committee on Computational Linguistics.

Yu-Hua Chen and Paul Baker. 2016. Investigating criterial discourse features across second language development: Lexical bundles in rated learner essays, cefr b1, b2 and c1. *Applied Linguistics*, 37(6):849–880.

Tino Didriksen. 2003. Constraint grammar manual: 3rd version of the cg formalism variant. ApS, GrammarSoft.

Thomas Gaillat, Andrew Simpkin, Nicolas Ballier, Bernardo Stearns, Annanda Sousa, Manon Bouyé, and Manel Zarrouk. 2022. Predicting cefr levels in learners of english: the use of microsystem criterial features in a machine learning approach. *ReCALL*, 34(2):130–146.

HABE. 2015. *Helduen Euskalduntzearen Oinarrizko Curriculuma*. HABE, Donostia.

Ana Cristina Lahuerta. 2018. Study of accuracy and grammatical complexity in efl writing. *International Journal of English Studies*, 18(1):71–89.

Chun Then Lim, Chih How Bong, Wee Sian Wong, and Nung Kion Lee. 2021. A comprehensive review of automated essay scoring (aes) research and development. *Pertanika Journal of Science & Technology*, 29(3):1875–1899.

Fabian Pedregosa, Gaël Varoquaux, Alexandre Gramfort, Vincent Michel, Bertrand Thirion, Olivier Grisel, Mathieu Blondel, Peter Prettenhofer, Ron Weiss, Vincent Dubourg, et al. 2011. Scikit-learn: Machine learning in python. *the Journal of machine Learning research*, 12:2825–2830.

Jennifer Thewissen. 2013. Capturing l2 accuracy developmental patterns: Insights from an error-tagged efl learner corpus. *The Modern Language Journal*, 97(S1):77–101.

Sowmya Vajjala and Kaidi Loo. 2014. Automatic cefr level prediction for estonian learner text. In *Proceedings of the third workshop on NLP for computer-assisted language learning*, pages 113–127.

Salvatore Valenti, Francesca Neri, and Alessandro Cucchiarelli. 2003. An overview of current research on automated essay grading. *Journal of Information Technology Education: Research*, 2(1):319–330.

Elena Volodina, Ildikó Pilán, David Alfter, et al. 2016. Classification of swedish learner essays by cefr levels. *CALL communities and culture–short papers from EUROCALL*, 2016:456–461.

Helen Yannakoudakis, Øistein E Andersen, Ardeshir Geranpayeh, Ted Briscoe, and Diane Nicholls. 2018. Developing an automated writing placement system for esl learners. *Applied Measurement in Education*, 31(3):251–267.

Iraide Zipitria, Ana Arruarte, and Jon A Elorriaga. 2010. Automatically grading the use of language in learner summaries. In *Proceedings of the 18th international conference on computers in education, Putrajaya, Malaysia*, pages 46–50.

Iraide Zipitria, Jon A Elorriaga, and Ana Arruarte. 2011. Corpus-based performance analysis for automatically grading use of language in essays. In *Artificial Intelligence in Education: 15th International Conference, AIED 2011, Auckland, New Zealand, June 28–July 2011 15*, pages 591–593. Springer.

Kaja Zupanc and Zoran Bosnic. 2016. Advances in the field of automated essay evaluation. *Informatica*, 39(4).

Supplementary material

	Basque rule	Translation to English
1	A1. Sintaxia. Aditz trinkoa	A1. Syntax. Synthetic verb
2	B2. Zenbatzaileak	B2. Quantifiers
3	A2. Sintaxia. Aditz-izena	A2. Syntax. Verbal noun
4	A2. Sintaxia. Indikatiboko orainaldia	A2. Syntax. Present indicative
5	C1. ADT	C1. Synthetic verb
6	B1. Juntadura	B1. Coordination
7	B1. Aditza	B1. Verb
8	B1. Zehaztugabeak	B1. Indeterminates
9	A2. Sintaxia. Aspektu burutua	A2. Syntax. Perfective aspect
10	B2. Izena	B2. Nouns
11	B2. Izenordainak	B2. Pronouns
12	A1. Sintaxia. Indikatibo orainaldia	A1. Syntax. Past indicative
13	A1. Izena. Biziduna	A1. Noun. Animate
14	A1. Izena. Berezia	A1. Proper noun
15	A1. Aditz iragankorra	A1. Transitive verb
16	A1. Sintaxia. Gertakizuna	A1. Syntax. Future
17	A1. Izen funtziozko menderakuntza	A1. Noun subordinate clauses
18	A2. Deklnabidea. Soziatiboa	A2. Sociative declension
19	B2. Galdetzaileak	B2. Interrogatives
20	A1. Elkartuak. Aurkaritzakoa	A1. Adversative
21	B1. Aditz-izena	B1. Verbal noun
22	A2. Sintaxia. Bakuna, baiezkoa	A2. Simple sentence, affirmative
23	A1. Deklinabidea. Instrumentala	A1. Instrumental declension
24	A1. Galdetzailea. Zergatik	A1. Interrogative why
25	A2. Sintaxia. Aspektu ezburutua	A2. Syntax. Imperfective aspect.
26	A1. Elkartuak. Hautakaria	A1. Disjunctive
27	A1. Galdetzailea. Zer	A1. Interrogative what
28	A2. Deklinabidea. Adlatiboa	A2. Adlative declension
29	C1. Graduatzaileak	C1. Grade particles
30	B2. Adberbioak	B2. Adverbs
31	A2. Deklinabidea. Inesiboa	A1. Inessive declension
32	B1. Menderakuntza. Zehar galdera	B1. Subordination. Indirect/reported question
33	A2. Deklinabidea. Partitiboa	A2. Partitive declension
34	C1. ADL	C1. Auxiliary verb
35	C1. Deklinabidea	C1. Declension
36	A1. Deklinabidea. Ergatiboa	A1. Ergative declension
37	A2. Deklinabidea. Genitibo edutezkoa	A2. Possessive genitive declension
38	A1. Elkartuak. Baldintza	A1. Conditional
39	B2. Indartuak	B2. Strengthened forms
40	A2. Sintaxia. Al partikula	A2. Syntax. Al particle
41	B1. Adberbioak	B1. Adverbs
42	A2. Deklinabidea. Genitibo leku-denborazkoa	A2. Declension. Spatiotemporal genitive
43	C1. Postposizioak	C1. Postpositions
44	B2. Postposizioak	B2. Postpositions
45	A1. Deklinabidea. Ablatiboa	A1. Ablative declension
46	C2. Modalizazioa	C2. Modalization
47	B2. Partikulak	B2. Particles
48	B1. Puntua laburduretan	B1. Dot in abbreviations
49	C1. Juntagailuak	C1. Conjunctions
50	C2. Testu-markatzaileak	C2. Text markers
51	B1. Plural hurbila	B1. Close plural
52	C1. Determinatzaile zehaztugabea	C1. Indefinite determiner
53	C1. Indartuak	C1. Strengthened forms
54	A2. Deklinabidea. Destinatiboa	A2. Destination declension
55	C1. Aditzak	C2. Verbs
56	B1. Deiktiko pertsonalak	B1. Personal deictics
57	C1 Moduzkoak1	C1. Modal clauses1
58	C1. Moduzkoak2	C1. Modal clauses2
59	B1. Elkarkariak	B1. Reciprocality
60	C1. Moduzkoak3	C1. Modal clauses3
61	C2. Operatzaile argudiozkoak	C2. Argumentative operators
62	C1. Testu-antolatzaileak	C1. Discourse markers
63	C1. Helburuzkoak	C1. Final clauses
64	C1. Kontzetsiboak	C1. Concessive
65	A1. Sintaxia. Ahalera	A1. Syntax. Potential
66	C2. Berbaldi markatzaileak	C2. Discourse markers
67	B2. Menderakuntza. Galde-perpausa	B2. Subordination. Question sentence
68	C1. Aditzondoak	C1. Mood adverbs
69	B2. Aditz lokuzioak	B2. Verbal locution
70	C1. Mendekoak	C1. Subordination

Correcting well-known interference errors – Towards a L2 grammar checker for Inari Saami

Trond Trosterud
The Arctic University of Norway
trond.trosterud
@uit.no

Marja-Liisa Olthuis
Oulu University
marja-liisa.olthuis
@oulu.fi

Linda Wiechetek
The Arctic University of Norway
linda.wiechetek
@uit.no

Abstract

We present *GramDivvun*, the first Inari Saami grammar checker for L2 users. The grammar checker is an important tool in the revitalisation of the language, in particular for strengthening the literary language. As the Inari Saami language community needs language tools predominantly for language learners, the focus is on grammatical interference errors made by (mostly Finnish-speaking) learners. Six of these errors are featured in the first version of the grammar checker. For non-proofread text written by inexperienced writers, precision is good, 73%. With experienced text and proofread text, alarms are rare but precision considerably lower, 19.5 % on average, but varying considerably between the error types. The paper discusses reasons for this variation. Future plans are improving results by means of increased testing, especially for complex sentences, and eventually also including more error types.

1 Introduction

Knowing what a language community needs is the basis for creating meaningful writing tools. In the Inari Saami case, most speakers at work age have learnt the language as adults, and now they are also taking great responsibility for creating modern writing culture, with linguistic help of a handful of native speakers. The next step is to write more and thereby becoming more proficient writers. In order to facilitate this, there is a need for writing tools for L2 users. According to feedback from L2 writers, they need a grammar checker to correct their own texts. The focus on the subsequent revision process can then be on errors outside the scope of both spell checker and grammar checker.

Modern language technology tools, in particular a spellchecker and a morphologically-aware e-dictionary, have been introduced to Inari Saami writers, and these tools are in active use. Based on Inari Saami proofreading experience, the most common type of errors is syntactic interference errors copying Finnish syntax, as described in chapter 3.

In order to help writers correct such errors, we have built a grammar checker for Inari Saami, *GramDivvun*, with L2 writers as its primary target group. The whole grammar checker is freely available on our web page and can be integrated in Google Docs and Microsoft Word as described on the web page. In this article we shall investigate whether *GramDivvun* for some specific constructions is able to change the grammatical structure in L2 writers' Inari Saami text from an underlying Finnish grammar to a correct Inari Saami one. At the same time *GramDivvun* should also be usable as an L1 speakers' grammar checker. In order to do this, we made a rule-based grammar checker for Inari Saami with the same technical framework as the ones for North Saami (Wiechetek et al., 2019) and Lule Saami (Mikkelsen et al., 2022), but where the focus was not on L1 but on L2 users.

Section 2 presents the language community and the technical background for the programs chosen. Section 3 discusses grammatical differences between Inari Saami and Finnish (the native language of most Inari Saami writers) and section 4 presents the grammar checker program. Then section 5 presents how the grammar checker deals with errors and evaluates its performance. Finally, in section 6 comes a conclusion.

2 Background

2.1 The language community

The Inari Saami language has been strongly revitalised since 1986. The focus of the revitalisation movement has initially been on oracy. The

https://divvun.no/korrektur/gramcheck.html

Proceedings of the NoDaLiDa 2023 Workshop on Constraint Grammar - Methods, Tools and Applications, pages 29–36
May 22, 2023

language has been revitalised by language nest activities and in schools as language of instruction (Olthuis et al., 2013). Also two intensive project-based language learning study years have been organised for working people. The CASLE programme took place in 2009-2010 and trained primarily teachers and nursery school teachers, but also journalists, clergy and civil servants. (Olthuis et al., 2013) The Agile University project trained teachers for all three Saami languages in Finland in 2019–2022: North, Inari and Skolt Saami. (Mattanen et al., 2023)

Especially during recent years, writing culture and written domains have been strengthened. Since 2015, writing tools have been developed by Divvun/Giellatekno at the Arctic university of Norway, UiT. That same year, a project for creating 100 writers for the Inari Saami language was born during the Inari Saami machine translation project in Tromsø, see (Morottaja et al., 2018) pp. 62-63 for a presentation. Since then, the language has gotten more visibility as a literary language. Now it has a communal magazine *Anarâš* (since 1987) and a youth magazine *Loostâš* (since 2020) which are published up to four times a year, see (Anarâškielâ servi, 2023). Furthermore, it has a brand-new e-newspaper, Anarâš aavis published since March 2023 by the Inari Saami association *Anarâškielâ servi* .

The association has the intention to publish 100 children's and youth books (Anarâškielâ servi, 2023), in the absence of Inari Saami language reading materials for these generations.

Text revision in the above mentioned writing domains shows the differences in the writing skills of the authors. The same observation has been done by (Morottaja et al., 2018) pp. 62. Some L2 writers are having difficulties with syntactic and grammatical structures. *GramDivvun* is mainly made for L2 writers, but should also avoid false alarms for L1 users.

The language community counts only a handful of L1 writers. In this group the speakers are mainly either elderly people or children after a strong language revitalisation movement. Elderly speakers have never learnt to write in their own language, and therefore, if they write something, they rather tend to use their own personal orthographies, being a less fruitful basis for developing spell-checkers

`https://www.anarasaavis.fi`
`https://anaraskielaservi.fi/`

(cf. (Morottaja et al., 2018)). The linguistic competence of L1-speakers is good, so the L2 speakers/writers can profit from their language skills in common. The students have the elderly speakers as language masters, in order to learn the daily spoken language fluently.

We argue that offering proofreading and writing support helps to increase the number of publications and motivates to write creatively and translate literature. The needed experience in reading and writing will come with time.

2.2 Technical background

The Inari Saami grammar checker and all its modules are part of a multilingual infrastructure *GiellaLT*, which includes 130 languages altogether.

The technological implementation of the grammar checker is based on finite-state automata for morphological analysis (Beesley and Karttunen, 2003; Lindén et al., 2013; Pirinen and Lindén, 2014) and constraint grammar for syntactic and semantic as well as other sentence-level processing. Constraint Grammar is a rule-based formalism for writing grammars that disambiguate and syntactically label text. It was initially presented by Fred Karlsson (Karlsson, 1990; Karlsson et al., 1995), we use the free open source implementation VISLCG-3 (Bick and Didriksen, 2015; Didriksen, 2016). The Inari Saami morphological analyser and lexicon is included in the *GiellaLT* infrastructure (Moshagen et al., 2013) and is publicly available .

The grammar checker is built on a pipeline of modules: we process the input text with morphological analysers and disambiguate and then apply grammar rules on the disambiguated sentences, as described above, c.f. Figure 1. The grammar checker takes this input and sends it to a number of other modules, the core of which are several Constraint Grammar modules for tokenisation disambiguation, morpho-syntactic disambiguation and a module for error detection and correction. The full modular structure is described in Wiechetek (2019).

2.3 Earlier research

Inari Saami is a language with agglutinative morphology combined with a rich array of stem changing processes, as shown in (Olthuis, 2000) and (Valtonen et al., 2022).

`https://github.com/giellalt/lang-smn`

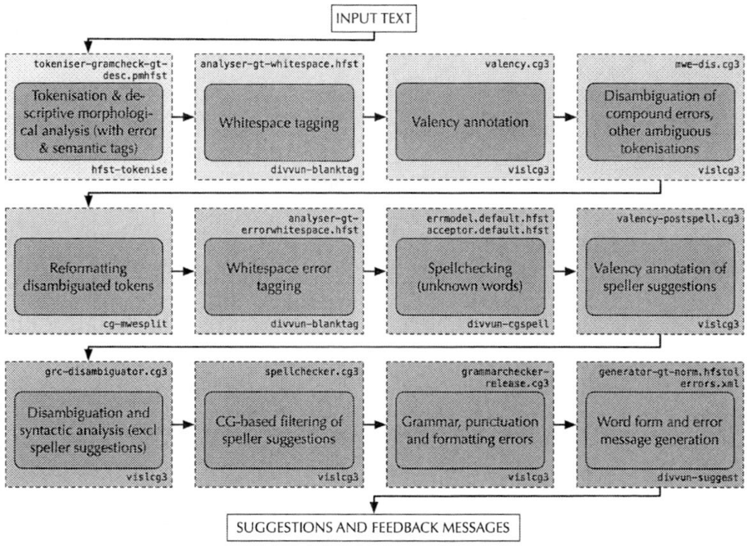

Figure 1: System architecture of the Inari Saami grammar checker (*GramDivvun*)

Work on Inari Saami language technology started out with a project on machine translation (Antonsen et al., 2017). This work also gave rise to a spellchecker (Morottaja et al., 2018).

L2 writers are known to make errors based upon Finnish interference, but there has so far not been published systematic research on the topic.

3 Grammatical error types

3.1 A typology of errors

Based upon our earlier experience, we assume that L2 speakers have only minor problems with orthography. Their major challenges are related to syntax (mainly interference from Finnish), morphosyntax and morphophonology.

As Inari Saami proofreading has shown, one of the most common error types are interference errors, as well as grammatical errors due to inflectional forms (especially case forms) being similar to each other.

Syntax errors are mainly interference errors, copying the Finnish syntax unchanged into Inari Saami. The syntactic structure of Finnish and Inari Saami are quite similar, but still different enough to give rise to a well-known set of interference errors. The main focus of the present grammar checker is upon these errors. At the same time, both L1 and L2 writers need the program to be robust enough to not give too many false alarms.

Given that the Inari Saami language community is small (appr. 450 speakers and even fewer writers), we have a very limited amount of written text at our disposal. We will still investigate to what extent it is possible to draw conclusions from it.

The following section shows a number of real-world error examples that have served as a basis for our error typology.

3.2 Object marking errors

In transitive sentences, the totality object in plural is in the nominative in Finnish (1), whereas the object case is only accusative in Inari Saami (2):

(1) Minä ostin kirjat.
I.NOM buy.1SG.PST book.PL.NOM
'I bought the books.'

(2) Mun ostim kiirjijd.
I.NOM buy.1SG.PST book.PL.ACC

(3) *Mun ostim kirjeh.
I.NOM buy.1SG.PST book.PL.NOM

The typical interference error for L2 writers is to use plural nominative also in Inari Saami, instead of the accusative, thus *kirjeh*, pro *kiirjijd*, as in (3). Furthermore, if the totality in Inari Saami needs to be stressed, it should be given by adding an attribute, like *puoh kiirjijd* 'all books' or *taid kiirjijd* 'those books'. In Inari Saami the use of accusative gives a perfect counterpart for the Finnish partial object in partitive (example (4)).

(4) Minä ostin kirjoja.
I.NOM buy.1SG.PST book.PL.PAR
'I bought some books.'

In negative sentences, the object case marking is again different: Where Finnish negative objects occur in partitive (5), the Inari Saami ones are not sensitive to negation, and occur in the genitive (in the Saami grammatical tradition called accusative)(6).

(5) Minä en ostanut kirjaa.
I.NOM NEG.1SG buy.PRFPTCP book.SG.PAR
'I did not buy any book.'

(6) Mun jiem uástám kirje.
I.NOM NEG.1SG buy.PTCPPRS book.SG.GEN
'I did not buy any book.'

Usually, these types of sentences do not cause any troubles for the L2 speaker.

In Finnish, the object can express completion (by using genitive) and incompletion (by using partitive) of a process, cf. (7) vs. (8):

(7) Minä luen kirjan.
I.NOM read.1PL.PRS book.PL.GEN
'I read the book.'

(8) Luen kirjaa.
read.1PL.PRS book.PL.PAR
'I am reading a/the book.'

The Inari Saami parallel of (7) is (9), with the object in genitive. The case is the same in the two languages, and there are no interference errors. The content in (8) should in Inari Saami be expressed with the present continuous, as in (10):

(9) Mun luuvâm kirje.
I.NOM read.1SG.PRS book.SG.GEN
'I read the book.'

(10) Mun lam luhâmin
I.NOM be.1SG.PRS read.1SG.PST.CONT.1SG
kirje.
book.SG.GEN
'I am reading a/the book.'

The different ways the two languages express incompleted action seems to cause problems for the L2 speakers.

Also the object of an imperative verb is often erroneously realised as plural nominative, modeled after Finnish *Osta sukset!* (11), instead of the correct accusative ((12)).

(11) *Uásti saveheh!
buy.IMP ski.PL.NOM
'Buy skis!'

(12) Uásti savehijd!
buy.IMP ski.PL.ACC
'Buy skis!'

3.3 Existential clauses and the habitive construction

The agreement pattern in existential clauses and habitive constructions shows several differences between Finnish and Inari Saami.

Firstly, interference occurs in E(xistential)-subject marking, for example where the Finnish plural partitive ((13)) is erroneously realised as accusative in prohibitions, like in the example (14), as compared to correct (15). In Finnish, the verb is in singular , whereas in Inari Saami the verb agrees with the E-subject.

(13) Minulla ei ole
I.LOC NEG.3SG/NEG.3PL be.CONNEG
ystäviä
friend.PL.PAR
'I have no friends'

(14) *Must ij/iä lah
I.LOC NEG.3SG/NEG.3PL be.CONNEG
ustevijd
friend.PL.ACC
'I have no friends'

(15) Must iä lah usteveh
I.LOC NEG.3PL be.CONNEG friend.PL.NOM
'I have no friends'

The same E-subject congruence also applies for the affirmative clauses, in both clause types, with (16) being the Finnish pattern, (17) the interference error (with accusative representing partitive and (18) being the correct Inari Saami form):

(16) Pihalla on koiria.
yard.ADE be.3SG.PRS dog.PL.PAR
'There are dogs in the yard.'

(17) *Šiljoost lii pennuid.
yard.LOC be.3SG.PRS dog.PL.ACC

(18) Šiljoost láá pennuuh.
yard.LOC be.3PL.PRS dog.PL.NOM
'There are dogs in the yard.'

Despite Inari Saami having a partitive case, it behaves different from its Finnish counterpart, and the case used during interference from Finnish in existential sentences is the accusative plural, *pennuid*. Also, the plural verbform *láá* is often replaced with the singular *lii*, as shown in (17). Some writers note the verb congruence but forget the e-subject in the accusative, though.

The grammar checker will target those errors.

4 The grammar checker

The Inari Saami grammar checker is built on hand-written Constraint Grammar rules. The grammar checker module uses mainly two syntactic rule types, *ADD* for adding error labels, and *COPY* for creating correct morphological strings that are then generated by the morphological *FST* generator. In this version of *GramDivvun*, we use flat syntactic structures, including valencies and semantic categories. There is an option for including dependencies if the specific error type requires it. However this has not been the case for the rules implemented for Inari Saami yet.

The simplified ADD-rule in the box below adds an error tag (&msyn-obj-plnom-placc) to a plural nominative noun if it has a left context with a transitive finite verb that is preceded by a nominative. We further exclude (with the *0C* condition) the possibility that the target noun has other readings than nominative plural. In addition we exclude that there is a third person plural verb in agreement with the noun to its right.

The COPY-rule on the other hand replaces the nominative tag with an accusative tag. In addition it removes the error tag and replaces it with the label &SUGGEST marking that this line is a correction of the error.

```
ADD (&msyn-obj-plnom-placc) TARGET N
IF
(*-1 VFIN + TV LINK -1 Nom)
(0C N + Pl + Nom)
(NOT *1 V + 3pl BARRIER NOT-ADV);

COPY (Acc &SUGGEST)
EXCEPT (Nom &msyn-obj-plnom-placc)
TARGET (N Pl &msyn-obj-plnom-placc);
```

The present version of the grammar checker contains 160 Constraint Grammar rules (dated 16.03.2023) that map error labels onto word forms, for 88 different error types. In this article we focus on a smaller selection of the most frequent error types that get corrected reliably without too many false alarms. The focus is on releasing a preliminary tool that can be tested by users.

The grammar checker is documented at `https://giellalt.github.io/lang-smn/tools-grammarcheckers-grammarchecker.cg3.html`, with link to the source code at the end of the document.

5 Evaluation

5.1 Test setup

For texts written by the target audience (language learners) we hand-picked uncorrected early versions of Wikipedia, written by L2 users, cf. 5.2.

We also looked at how the grammar checker copes with texts written by more experienced writers. For that, we evaluated some 1,27 million words, and got 227 relevant alarms. These alarms are evaluated in section 5.3 below.

5.2 Evaluation of the L2 results

Table 1 illustrates the results. The false positives are unsuccessful corrections. However, 7 of the 9 instances are successful error detections.

	interference corp
TP	24
FN	95
FP	9
Precision	72.73%
Recall	20.17%

Table 1: Evaluation of the Inari Saami grammar checker

The quality is measured using basic precision, recall and f_1 scores, such that recall $R = \frac{t_p}{t_p+f_n}$, precision $P = \frac{t_p}{t_p+f_p}$ and f_1 score as harmonic mean of the two: $F_1 = 2\frac{P \times R}{P+R}$, where t_p is a count of true positives, f_p false positives, t_n true negatives and f_n false negatives.

The qualitative evaluation of the results is shown in table 1. Looking at some of the examples, we se in ex. (19) a case error in the subject *čuoigâmkammuuh* (nominative plural should be accusative). This case error disrupts the agreement between the presumable plural subject (which should be an object) and the third person singular verb *koolgâi*. The grammar checker finds that there is an error in the sentence, but instead of fixing the case error it suggests an error in the verb form *koolgâi*. Even though this counts as a false alarm, *GramDivvun* is successful in error detection in general.

(19) Máttáátteijee čielgij, maht
teacher.SG.NOM explain.3SG.PST, what
čuoigâmkammuuh koolgâi
skishoe.PL.NOM should.3SG.PST
kiddiđ saveháid.
fasten.INF ski.PL.ILL

'The teacher explained how the ski shoes should be fastened to the ski.'

Also in the next sentence, the verb *koolgâi* is corrected by GramDivvun instead of the nominative plural noun *oppâkirjeh*.

(20) Talle oppâkirjeh koolgâi
then textbook.PL.NOM should.3SG.PST
jurgâliđ suomâkielâst sämikielân.
translate.INF Finnish.SG.LOC Saami.ILL
'Then the text books needed to be translated from Finnish into Saami'

Here, case errors as in *kuobbâreh*, which should be *kuobbârijd* (Acc Pl), and *tábáhtusâid* (N Pl Acc corrected to nominative msyn-extsubj-acc-nom), which should be *tábáhtusah*, are identified correctly.

(21) Nubeh tobdeh kuobbâreh
others identify.3PL mushroom.PL.NOM
ivneest.
colour.LOC
'Others identify mushrooms by their colour.'

(22) Mist láá eenâb-uv tábáhtusâid.
I.LOC be.3SG.PRS more event.PL.ACC
'We have even more events than that.'

5.3 Presicion evaluation of proofread, published texts

In order to evaluate precision we ran a test on a larger corpus of blogs, news and science texts. These texts were proofread and published. The size of test corpus was appr. 1.27 million words. The total number of alarms for the relevant error types was 169. The result was as shown in table 2 . As can be seen, the result of this second evaluation deviates strongly from the first test.

Error type	TP	FP	Precision
Ext. verb 3sg → 3pl	9	2	81.0 %
Ext. verb 3pl → 3sg	15	43	25.9 %
E-subj acc → nom	5	45	10.0 %
E-subj gen → nom	4	46	8.0 %
Overall precision	33	136	19.5 %

Table 2: Evaluation of Inari Saami *GramDivvun* on a corpus of news and science texts (N=1266071)

The best result (81 %) was provided by the rule set correcting singular existential verbs from 3sg into 3pl. For the false alarms of the type 3sg → 3pl, the rule failed to identify the clause boundary between singular *lii* and plural *virgeomâháách*.

(23) Olgoštem muuneeldestim
discrimination prevention.SG.GEN
táához lii tehálâš,
perspective.SG.LOC be.3PL.PRS important,
et virgeomâháách já palvâlusfälleeh
that official.PL.NOM and servant.PL.NOM
ovdedeh toimâidis
promote.3PL.PRS activity.ACC.PX3PL
oovtviärdásâžžân já pasteh tarvaniđ meid
equalESS
olgošteijee tooimân.

'From the point of view of preventing discrimination, it is important that public authorities and service providers promote equality and are able to tackle discriminatory behaviour.'

For the opposite correction, 3pl → 3sg, the results were somewhat worse. It seems advanced writers have several ways of expressing plural referents, ways that are not captured by the grammar checker.

In (24), the problem was a wrongly disambiguated *anarâškielâ*. The word could be either nominative or genitive, but since it was disambiguated as nominative, the grammar checker errouneously corrected the plural verb *láá* to singular *lii*, despite the subsequent plural form *uáppeeh*.

(24) škoovlâst láá uđđâ
school.SG.LOC be.3PL.PRS new
anarâškielâ uáppeeh..
Inari.Saami.SG.GEN pupil.PL.NOM
'In the school, there are new Inari Saami pupils'

In (25), the problem is again an error of disambiguation. The time expression *manuppaje* has erroneously lost its genitive analysis, and as a perceived nominative singular it blocks for the reference to the correct subject *čielgiittâsah*.

(25) Taan kalenderist láá kevttum
this calendar be.3PL.PRS used
mánuppaje kuobbârist
month.SG.GEN mushroom.PL.LOC
siämmáálágán čielgiittâsah ko
similar explanation.PL.NOM as
oovdeld mainâšum
before mentioned
kuobârkirjeest-uv.
mushroom.book.SG.LOC.FOC
'This calendar uses the same explanations

TP = true positives, FP = false positives, Precision = TP/(TP+FP)

of the mushroom of the month as the fungus book mentioned above.'

The authors of the larger test corpus often used complex noun phrases, such as the coordination NP in (26), or the apposition *maailmist* following the quantor phrase in (27).

(26) Čielgâsávt stuárráámus uási Island
clearly largest part Iceland
tuálvumist láá kyeli já
income.SG.LOC be.3PL.PRS fish.SG.NOM and
kyelipyevtittâsah.
fish.product.PL.NOM
'The largest part of Icelands income clearly consists of fish and fish products.'

(27) [m]aŋgâ kielâ maailmist
many language.SG.GEN world.SG.LOC
láá lappum
be.3PL.PRS disappear.PTC
'Many languages of the world have disappeared'

Removing *maailmist* from the quantor phrase would have removed the false alarm. The improvement needed is thus to take such appositions into account.

A recurrent phenomenon in the experienced writers' corpus was the use of third person plural pro-drop, like in (28):

(28) Tommittáá tast láá
so.much that.ADV.LOC be.3PL.PRS
sárnum já čáállám sehe
talk.PTCPPRS and write.PTCPPRS both
sämi já lädimediast.
Sámi and Finnish.media.SG.LOC
'So much about this people have talked and written both in Sámi and Finnish media.'

This phenomenon is not common in Finnish and has thus not been present in the learner corpus on which the grammar checker development has been focused.

Topicalised e-subjects like the one shown in (29) were rarely encountered in the learner corpus and thus not within the range of the grammar checker rule set. In the reference corpus there were several instances of it.

(29) Kommemainâseh-uv sust
ghost.story.PL.NOM.FOC s/he.SG.LOC
láá, veikkâ ij tain poollâđ
be.3PL.PRS, although not.3SG that fear.INF
taarbâš.
need.CONNEG
'Ghost stories s/he has, even though one does not need to be afraid of them'

The grammar checker also has not taken into account listing of referents following a colon. Cf. (30).

(30) Sii lasseen ive 2018
they in.addition.to year 2018
kielâpiervâlijn láá porgâm:
language.nest.PL.LOC be.3PL.PRS work.PTC:
Tarja Passi, Tiina Lehmuslehti,
T.P., T.L.,
Minna Lampinen, ...
M.L., ...
'In addition to (the before mentioned), in the year 2018 the following people have worked in the language nests: T.P., T.L., M.L., ...'

List formatting such as the one in (30) was not encountered in the learner corpus, hence the grammar checker did not take them into account.

The poorest results were found for the errors correcting e-subject case errors. Here, a recurrent problem was complex sentences with several NPs following the existential sentence proper. The grammar checker targeted simple sentence constructions and failed to identify barriers to prevent it from errouneously flagging the right dislocated NPs as subject errors. (31) is a case in point.

(31) [A]narâškielâ várás iä lah
Inari.Saami for not.3PL be.CONNEG
kielâtotkei virgeh, já nuuvt
linguist.PL.GEN position.PL.NOM, and thus
jieškote-uv totkee ferttee kavnâđ
each researcher must find
vuovijd maht ruttâdiđ jieijâs
way.PL.ACC that finance ones.own
projektijd já pargoid.
projects and works
'There are no permanent linguist positions for Inari Saami, and thus each and every researcher must find a way to finance his or her projects and work.'

6 Conclusion and future perspectives

We have written a basic Inari Saami grammar checker (*GramDivvun*). Here we evaluate a subset of if, containing rules for the 5 most common error types of L2 users. Based on our evaluation of a test corpus of learner texts, the subset of L2 error rules presented in section 3 has a fairly good precision of 73% This corpus had a high number of interference errors, and the grammar checker was able to identify them quite reliably. Compared to this, the precision in a larger reference corpus written by more experienced writers was lower.

The grammar checker focuses on interference errors from Finnish. The experience from the present study indicates that the focus for some time to come should be upon improving precision for the rules discussed in the present paper, with a focus on recall being the next step. Investigating other error types in Inari Saami text and correcting them we leave for further research.

7 Bibliographical References

References

Anarâškielâ servi. 2023. Anarâškielâ servi publications. `https://anaraskielaservi.fi/Almostitmeh/`.

Lene Antonsen, Ciprian Gerstenberger, Maja Kappfjell, Sandra Nystø Rahka, Marja-Liisa Olthuis, Trond Trosterud, and Francis M. Tyers. 2017. Machine translation with North Saami as a pivot language. In *Proceedings of the 21st Nordic Conference on Computational Linguistics, NoDaLiDa, 22–24 May 2017, Gothenburg, Sweden*, volume 29 of *NEALT Proceedings Series*, pages 123–131. Linköping University Electronic Press.

Kenneth R Beesley and Lauri Karttunen. 2003. Finite-state morphology: Xerox tools and techniques. *CSLI, Stanford.*

Eckhard Bick and Tino Didriksen. 2015. CG-3 — beyond classical constraint grammar. In *Proceedings of the 20th Nordic Conference of Computational Linguistics (NODALIDA 2015)*, pages 31–39, Vilnius, Lithuania. Linköping University Electronic Press, Sweden.

Tino Didriksen. 2016. *Constraint Grammar Manual: 3rd version of the CG formalism variant*. GrammarSoft ApS, Denmark.

Fred Karlsson. 1990. Constraint grammar as a framework for parsing running text. In *COLING '90 Proceedings of the 13th conference on Computational linguistics*, volume 3, pages 168–173, Helsinki.

Fred Karlsson, Atro Voutilainen, Juha Heikkilä, and Arto Anttila. 1995. *Constraint Grammar: A Language-Independent System for Parsing Unrestricted Text*. Mouton de Gruyter, Berlin.

Krister Lindén, Erik Axelson, Senka Drobac, Sam Hardwick, Juha Kuokkala, Jyrki Niemi, Tommi A Pirinen, and Miikka Silfverberg. 2013. Hfst—a system for creating nlp tools. In *International workshop on systems and frameworks for computational morphology*, pages 53–71. Springer.

Tiina Mattanen, Marja-Liisa Olthuis, Anni-Siiri Länsman, and Sari Harmoinen. 2023. Máŋggahámat skuvlen oassečoavddusin sámegielat ávnnasoahpaheaddjiid váilumii. *Dutkansearvvi dieđalaš áigečála*, 7(1):6–30.

Inga Lill Sigga Mikkelsen, Linda Wiechetek, and Flammie A Pirinen. 2022. Reusing a multi-lingual setup to bootstrap a grammar checker for a very low resource language without data. In *Proceedings of the Fifth Workshop on the Use of Computational Methods in the Study of Endangered Languages*, pages 149–158, Dublin, Ireland. Association for Computational Linguistics.

Petter Morottaja, Marja-Liisa Olthuis, Trond Trosterud, and Lene Antonsen. 2018. Anarâškielâ tivvoomohjelm – kielâ- já ortografiafeeilâi kuorrâm tivvoomohjelmáin. *Dutkansearvvi dieđalaš áigečála*, 1(2):63–84.

Sjur N. Moshagen, Tommi A. Pirinen, and Trond Trosterud. 2013. Building an open-source development infrastructure for language technology projects. In *NODALIDA*.

Marja-Liisa Olthuis. 2000. *Kielâoppâ. Inarinsaamen kielioppi*. Sämitigge, Inari.

Marja-Liisa Olthuis, Suvi Kivelä, and Tove Skutnabb-Kangas. 2013. *Revitalising Indigenous Languages. How to recreate a lost Generation?* Multilingual Matters, Bristol.

Tommi Pirinen and Krister Lindén. 2014. State-of-the-art in weighted finite-state spell-checking. In *Computational Linguistics and Intelligent Text Processing : 15th International Conference on Intelligent Text Processing and Computational Linguistics, CICLing 2014, Kathmandu, Nepal, April 6-12, 2014, Proceedings, Part II*, volume 2, pages 519–532, Berlin Heidelberg. Springer-Verlag.

Taarna Valtonen, Jussi Ylikoski, and Luobbal Sámmol Sámmol Ánte (Ante Aikio). 2022. 178Aanaar (Inari) Saami. In *The Oxford Guide to the Uralic Languages*. Oxford University Press.

Linda Wiechetek, Sjur Nørstebø Moshagen, Børre Gaup, and Thomas Omma. 2019. Many shades of grammar checking – launching a constraint grammar tool for North Sámi. In *Proceedings of the NoDaLiDa 2019 Workshop on Constraint Grammar - Methods, Tools and Applications*, NEALT Proceedings Series 33:8, pages 35–44.

Supporting Language Users – Releasing the first Lule Sámi Grammar Checker

Inga Lill Sigga Mikkelsen
UiT Norgga árktalaš universitehta
inga.l.mikkelsen@uit.no

Linda Wiechetek
UiT Norgga árktalaš universitehta
linda.wiechetek@uit.no

Abstract

We present the first rule-based L1 grammar checker for Lule Sámi. Releasing a Lule Sámi grammar checker has direct consequences for language revitalization. Our primary intention is therefore to support language users in their writing and their confidence to use the language. We release a version of the tool for MS Word and GoogleDocs that corrects six grammatical error types. For the benefit of the user, the selection of error types is based on frequency of the errors and the quality of our tool. Our most successful error correction, for a phonetically and syntactically motivated copula error, reaches a precision of 96%.

1 Introduction

We release a new L1 grammar correction tool for Lule Sámi that can be integrated in MS Word and GoogleDocs. *GramDivvun* is the first grammar checker for Lule Sámi and has been released May 31st 2023.[1] The underlying purpose is to provide a tool that can give language users the security that their language is right in the absence of a strict norm - a paradox we face in our daily work. Speakers and writers of a language are confident and carefree when they feel secure in their language use.[2] However, minority languages often face loss of language arenas and at the same time have less resources for language teaching than majority languages. The consequence is that (new) language users get insecure in their use of language and are often left to criticism by the language experts when speaking or writing. This can lead to frustration and resistance to use the language among the ones that are not considered language experts. The notion of the language barrier - where older generations take the role of the 'language police' - has also been reported in other indigenous language contexts, for example when learning the Cree language as an adult. (McCreery, 2006, pp.43) (Johansen, 2006)

As one of the authors of this work is herself a member of the Lule Sámi speech community she is familiar with general attitudes, one of which is that the ones that know the language have a clear feeling of how the language should be, even if there is not a written norm. This creates a gap between these experts and the language learners. At the same time there are few contexts/opportunities to improve one's grammar skills and avoid being criticised so that speaking can lead to anxiety and speakers can feel discouraged to use the language. Especially in writing, Lule Sámi text production differs from its coexisting majority language text production. Even official texts and texts written by highly proficient users contain a lot of spelling and grammar errors (Wiechetek et al., 2022). This is due to lower written language proficiency in minority languages, and also a lack of written norms.

A norm and someone enforcing this norm is necessary to teach language competence to the younger generation and pass on expert language knowledge in all its richness. In the absence of sufficient L1 teachers, now many L2 speakers are becoming teachers that need support to teach the language in all its details. There are no books that explain grammatical phenomena in all their details, including contrasting examples and frequent mistakes. Existing grammar books only have text book examples and focus on morphology, rather than syntax. Where sufficient human feedback on our language production is missing, we need a tool that can evaluate the correctness our language on the fly.

[1] https://divvun.no/en/korrektur/gramcheck.html

[2] "A positive attitude is also connected with creating a safe environment for learners." (McCreery, 2006)

Proceedings of the NoDaLiDa 2023 Workshop on Constraint Grammar - Methods, Tools and Applications, pages 37–45
May 22, 2023

Our language technology tools already have a wide user base including official domains such as the Sámi Parliament, Sámi media and schools that use our proofreading tools. The grammar checker will be included in the automatic updates of future versions of the spellchecker to provide better tools for the users. *Divvun* has been established to provide language technology tools for the Sámi language community, and has an ownership agreement with the Sámi Parliament, which unequivocally states that what Divvun develops belongs to the Sámi people through the Sámi Parliament.

The construction of a Lule Sámi grammar checker started in October 2020 with a general error categorization and smaller experiments with rules. In 2022 we did intensive work to collect regression tests and reported first results (Mikkelsen et al., 2022). The main motivation for making proofing tools are the needs of the language users and the tools' usability. That means that we want to make the tools available at an early stage, even if they do not include all the functionalities yet, and at the same time ensure their quality (i.e. especially good precision). Ensuring the quality means that only those error types that give a certain precision are included. The tools are meant to support teachers, proof readers and individuals by finding errors that are hard to detect because of orthographic similarities. They are also meant to help enforcing the (mostly orthographic) language norm proposed by the normative organ Giellagálldo[3] in a consistent way.

2 Language situation for Lule Sámi

Lule Sámi is an indigenous language spoken in Northern Norway and Sweden. The language is classified as a severely endangered language by UNESCO and has an estimated 800-3,000 speakers (Sammallahti, 1998; Kuoljok, 2002; Svonni, 2008; Rydving, 2013; Moseley, 2010). Lule Sámi is a morphologically complex language, for more details see Ylikoski (2022).

The current orthography of Lule Sámi was approved in 1983, and the first spell checker for the language was launched in 2007. Lule Sámi lacks a long written tradition. According to Kuoljok (1997) most of the speakers can barely read and even fewer write. This situation has changed since 1997. In the education system, Lule Sámi is taught and used as the language of instruction. In Norway, Lule Sámi was for the first time taught as first language in primary school in 1992, and from 2012 it was possible to take a bachelor's degree in Lule Sámi at Nord University. Lule Sámi is also to a greater extent used in public administration, in 2000 the Jåhkåmåhke/Jokkmokk municipality became one of the municipalities in Sweden with a Sámi-language administration and in 2006 the municipality Divtasvuona/Tysfjord was included in Norways Sámi-language administration municipalities. This development means that Lule Sámi is also used in writing to a greater extent than before. However, the written tradition is not very established, and the elderly heritage speakers master the written language only to a smaller extent.

In 2013, a Lule Sámi corpus of writing errors was created to test the spell checker's effectiveness. Today this corpus consist of 39,892 words, written by native Lule Sámi speakers, and it has all together 4,784 writing errors. 2,055 are nonword errors identified by the spell checker, while the remaining 2,729 errors are morpho-syntactic, syntactic and lexical errors that only a grammar checker can detect and correct (Wiechetek et al., 2022). The mark-up of this corpus shows an error rate of 11,9% in written texts, which indicates that Lule Sámi speakers struggle when writing the language.

To fully master a written language one must read a lot (Trosterud, 2021), minority language users therefore have a greater need for help in the writing process, since they do not experience their language in written form as much as majority language speakers. With Lule Sámi classified as a severely endangered language by UNESCO, it is important to increase the use of Lule Sámi to revitalize the language. A grammar checker for Lule Sámi would make it easier for people to write in the language, thus increasing its written use.

To develop a functional Lule Sámi grammar checker, we opted to focus on errors made by proficient speakers instead of second language learners. This approach allows us to create a grammar checker that can handle sentences with fewer errors and gradually introduce more complex errors. A grammar checker for texts written by second language learners would require a different approach as they tend to have more and different types of errors, including more complex errors.

Errors made by high proficiency speakers often arise when the written norm deviates from the spo-

[3] http://www.giella.org

ken dialectal variation or the "errors" might express an ongoing language change.

3 Technical background

All tools described in this article are part of a multilingual infrastructure for 130 languages (Moshagen et al., 2013).

Lule Sámi has a morphological analyser and lexicon, which are both publicly available[4]. The morphological analyser was originally imported with all rules and set specifications from North Sámi and then adapted to Lule Sámi.

GramDivvun takes input from the finite-state transducer (*FST*) to a number of other modules, the core of which are several Constraint Grammar modules for tokenisation disambiguation, morpho-syntactic disambiguation and a module for error detection and correction. The full modular structure is described in Wiechetek (2019). We are using finite-state morphology (Beesley and Karttunen, 2003) to model word formation processes. The technology behind our *FSTs* is described in Pirinen (2014). Constraint Grammar is a rule-based formalism for writing disambiguation and syntactic annotation grammars (Karlsson, 1990; Karlsson et al., 1995). In our work, we use the free open source implementation VISLCG-3 (Bick and Didriksen, 2015).

The challenge consists in writing rules that are as general as possible so one rule can cover many different erroneous forms at once. Most Lule Sámi grammatical errors can be referred to as a combination of morphological features that is confused with another combination, rather than a confusion pair of two lemmata as is typical for languages with less morphological complexity like English (e.g. *theirs–there's*). This allows for a higher degree of abstraction.

The syntactic context is specified in hand-written Constraint Grammar rules. The ADD-rule below adds an error tag (`&real-negSg3-negSg2`) to the negation auxiliary *ij* '(to) not (do)' as in example (1) if it is a 3rd person singular verb and to its left there is a 2nd person singular pronoun in the nominative case. The context condition further specifies a barrier for the rule to apply. Subjunctions, conjunctions, or finite verbs – typically indicating a new clause – stop the scanning of the rule.

Each ADD-rule is accompanied by a COPY-rule that exchanges relevant morphological tags in order to produce the correct sequence for the FST morphological generator to generate the correct form. In this case *Sg3* is exchanged for *Sg2*. At the same time, we add a tag, *&SUGGEST* to mark that this is not the erroneous form anymore, but the correction.

(1) Dån **ittjij** boade guossáj.
you.2SG NEG.PAST.3SG come guest.ILL
'You didn't visit.'

```
ADD (&real-negSg3-negSg2) TARGET ("ij")
IF (0 (Sg3))
(*-1 (Pron Nom Sg2)
BARRIER S-BOUNDARY OR
CS OR CC OR VFIN) ;

COPY (Sg2 &SUGGEST) EXCEPT (Sg3)
TARGET  (&real-NegSg3-NegSg2) ;
```

4 Lule Sámi Grammar checker

4.1 Testset

Having a set of example sentences that show the natural context for a grammatical error is essential for the construction of a grammar checker. We want to correct errors that are actually made by users of the language.

We have collected sentences and made regression tests of representative errors in *Yaml*-formatted[5] files specific to each error type. (Wiechetek et al., 2021) Typically, each regression file contains several hundred sentences. Our standard has been to have yaml tests of at least 50 test sentences. There should be a balance of correct and erroneous sentences covering the same phenomena so that one can test for false positives and false negatives. Test sentences should cover a variety of syntactic contexts and pay attention to long-distance relationships between syntactic functions. The sentence collection is designed to cover a maximally large amount of real-world errors that people make when writing texts, in order to keep the grammar checker usable for people. The file naming is now error-specific,[6] but as they come from an authentic corpus, they can contain multiple errors per sentence including other types of errors and nested errors.

[4] https://github.com/giellalt/lang-smj/

[5] https://yaml.org/spec/1.2/spec.html

[6] https://github.com/giellalt/lang-smj/tree/main/tools/grammarcheckers/tests

At first, we wrote test sentences for yaml tests ourselves and also searched SIKOR (SIKOR) manually for sentences with similar errors. After having written rules, we automatically harvested test sentences corrected by *GramDivvun* in the developer-corpus [7], and used these to improve the rules. At first, we wrote test sentences for yaml tests ourselves and also searched SIKOR manually for sentences with similar errors. After having written rules, we automatically harvested test sentences corrected by *GramDivvun* in the developer-corpus [8], and used these to improve the rules.

Yaml is a mark-up language with a simple syntax that makes writings of the tests convenient and co-operation with programmers and linguists easier [9]. We chose to use the Yaml format for grammar testing because of positive experiences with the use of the same format for spell checker testing.[10]

4.2 Grammar for error correction

It is challenging to write a prescriptive grammar checker for a language without a clear written norm. Even written grammar books of Lule Sámi do not cover all grammatical phenomena. Oral Lule Sámi contains a lot of dialectal variations and is subject to ongoing language change. As all speakers of Lule Sámi are bilingual, oral language can include interference and loans from the majority languages, which is not desired in a written norm. For all these reasons, it is a challenge to build a grammar checker that corrects this language. We face the question of where to put the boundaries between written and oral Lule Sámi. The decision can have serious consequences since Lule Sámi is an endangered language under revitalisation, and the grammar checker can have a standardising effect on the language of the younger generations. It is positive that speakers receive feedback when they write language that is clearly influenced by Norwegian or Swedish, but at the same time the grammar checker can also be thought to give feedback leading to a limitation of dialectal variation.

We do not have the authority to determine the norm, but with the release of the grammar checker, we might have the strongest influence regarding the sentence level norm in the entire Lule Sámi language community. One cannot wait until normative matters are solved before developing tools needed by the language community, the path must be created as we walk. The grammar checker will be further developed and improved after this first version release. Hopefully, the release of the Lule Sámi grammar checker will facilitate discussions around the norm and discussion around the choices made by us. Upon the release of the grammar checker, we had a presentations for the language community where we informed about the choices regarding the grammar checker and also discussed further development.

We have written 18 rule types, and from the evaluation six of these were ready to be released.

The words *oahpásmuvvat* and *oahpástuvvat* both meaning *to get to know* are often confused. The distinction lies in the animacy of what one is getting to know. *getting to know.* The verb *oahpásmuvvat*, in ex. (2) is used in inanimate contexts and requires illative case, whilst *oahpástuvvat*, in ex. (3) is used in animate context and require comitative case. The rules of the grammar checker corrects both verb according to animacy and the case of the referent.

(2) Oahpásmuváv bijllaj.
get.to.know.PRES.1SG car.SG.ILL
'I get to know the car.'

(3) Oahpástuváv sujna.
get.to.know.PRES.1SG PRON.2SG.COM
'I get to know her/him.'

The modal verb *soajttet* meaning 'maybe' should be paired with the infinitive form of the main verb. However, many writers are using the present singular third-person form *soajttá* as an adverb rather than a modal verb, as shown in ex. (4). In this example, the modal auxiliary is not followed by an infinitive as expected, but rather by a finite verb in the first-person singular form. The rules of the grammar checker will replace *soajttá* with the adverb *ihkap*. This correction is in line with the writer's intended adverb construction. An alternative to that would be inflecting *soajttá* according to

[7] https://giellalt.github.io/proof/gramcheck/extracting-precision-sentences.html
[8] https://giellalt.github.io/proof/gramcheck/extracting-precision-sentences.html
[9] The original test framework for morphology testing initiated by Brendan Molloy can be found on GitHub: https://github.com/apertium/apertium-tgl-ceb/blob/master/dev/verbs/HfstTester.py
[10] https://giellalt.uit.no/infra/infraremake/AddingMorphologicalTestData.html\#Yaml+tests

person and number of the subject and changing the following finite verb to an infinitive form. As this bears more risks in correction, especially when the subject is distant from the verb or dropped, we chose to replace the verb with an adverb.

(4) ***Soajttá** *tjálláv nágin
maybe.PRES.3SG write.PRES.1SG some
bágojt
word.SG.ACC
'Maybe I will write some words'

For agreement the grammar checker corrects relative pronouns in inessive case, as the incorrect ex. (5), and the reflexive pronouns *iesj* in nominative, as the incorrect ex. (6), when these do not agree with their anaphora in number. The grammar checker also corrects agreement errors between subject and verb, this is a quite common error done since indicative verbs are inflected for three numbers and three persons.

(5) Álu l má ålmmåjn ***gænna** l
often is PCLE man.PL.INE who.SG.INE have
fábmo
power
'Often it is men who have power'

(6) Mij hæhttup ***iesj**
we.NOM must.PRES.1PL self.REFL.SG.NOM
jáhkket
believe.
'We ourselves must believe.'

Another noun phrase internal error corrected by the grammar checker is the use of an attributive adjective in predicative position, as the incorrect ex. (7).

(7) Ássje l ***gássjelis** munji.
matter is difficult.ADJ.ATTR I.ILL
'The matter is difficult for me.'

For the copula verb *liehket* 'to be' the grammar checker has three different rule types following the system described in Spiik (1989). In sentence-initial position, the copulas have different forms from sentence internal forms, as shown for the present tense in Table 1. Even if this system is explained in (Spiik, 1989), the sentence internal forms are widely used sentence-initially in written texts, and the sentence initial 3. singular forms in both present and past tense are frequently used in sentence internal position. The sentence internal present 3. person singular form also varies between *la* or *l*: *la* is used if the preceding word ends on a consonant, and *l* is used if the preceding word ends on a vowel. Even though there most likely is and has been been dialectal variation in regarding the copula system, we have made rules according to Spiik (1989). We have even fine-tuned the rules for choosing between *la* or *l* since it really is not as straight forward as Spiik (1989) explains it. As developers we are not sure of how well copula correction will be received in the language community. The copula system of the grammar checker is not widely used in texts, for example, the translators of the Lule Sámi New Testament have chosen a different approach to the copula *liehket*. As the grammar checker allows users to turn off and on error types they want to have checked, they can turn certain corrections off, if they find them annoying.

Morphological form	Sentence internal	Sentence initial
1Sg	lav	lev
2Sg	la	le
3Sg	la/l	le
1Du	lin	len
2Du	lihppe	læhppe
3Du	libá	læbá
1Pl	lip	lep
2Pl	lihpit	lehpit
3Pl	li	le

Table 1: Paradigm for liehket 'to be'

5 Evaluation

For the evaluation of our tool, we use a part of *SIKOR*, the Lule Sámi corpus, containing administrative, law, religious, non-fiction, fiction, and science texts. SIKOR consists of a freely available corpus, *FREECORPUS*, and a corpus that is restricted by copyright, *BOUNDCORPUS*. We distinguish between three different parts: 1. the gold corpus for evaluation, marked-up for spelling and grammar errors, 2. the unmarked testing corpus and 3. the development corpus for developing rules. For simplicity, we will refer to the error marked-up gold corpus as *FREECORPUS* and *BOUNDCORPUS*. This work includes testing for inconsistencies and improvement of the manual grammar error mark-up the first time. Since the goldcorpus consists of text that has not been proof read, there are a lot of grammatical errors. The goldcorpus and its mark-up is described in

Wiechetek et al. (2022).

The testcorpus is not manually marked-up, but put aside for future evaluation and quality assurance as mark-up as the current goldcorpus is still fairly small, and needs enhancement to cover all different grammatical error types sufficiently. The development corpus on the other hand, is being used to test and improve the grammar checker rules on the fly. It is therefore not marked-up.

A preliminary evaluation on *BOUNDCORPUS* in Table 2 served to chose the error types to be included in the first version of *GramDivvun* and improve error mark-up in the gold corpus. Quality is measured using basic precision and recall, such that recall $R = \frac{t_p}{t_p+f_n}$, and precision $P = \frac{t_p}{t_p+f_p}$, where t_p is a count of true positives, f_p false positives, t_n true negatives and f_n false negatives.

	Precison	Recall	# Err
Copula forms	96.13%	83.71%	117
Rel agreement	72.22%	81.25%	17
soajttá as Adv	100.00%	100.00%	2
Refl agree	60.67%	33.33%	3
Animacy - Rel	33.33%	25.00%	3
oahpásmuvvat	100.00%	100.00%	1
Attr > Pred	0%	-	1
Pred > Attr	80.00%	40.00%	10
Subj-V agree	77.42%	25.53%	31
Num agree	60.00%	100.00%	10
Pass/Act	0%	0%	5

Table 2: Evaluation on *BOUNDCORPUS*

Table 2 shows that some error types have very few instances in *BOUNDCORPUS*. Some of this does not coincide with our manual proofreading experience and knowledge of frequent errors in written texts, and it may not reflect the real distribution of errors in a larger corpus either. Therefore, we use regression test results in Table 3 as a second criterion to select the error types for *GramDivvun*.

Based on the results of Tables 2 and 3, and keeping the quality assurance for the users in mind, we have released functionalities for errors regarding copula form and relative pronoun agreement, the second of which we reduced to errors regarding inessive case relative pronoun agreement. The first two error types have a good precision and perform well in regression testing. All of them have a precision above 70%. In addition, we have released error correction for error types with few instances

	PASS	FAIL
Copula form	122	7
Inessive rel number agreement	136	7
Modal verb *soajttá* as adverb	84	0
Refl number agreement	114	5
oahpásmuvvat-oahpástuvvat	63	1
Adjective form (Attr>Pred)	164	5
Subject-verb agreement	129	108
Past tense negation	46	8
Animacy of rel pronouns	140	63
Nominalization > finite verb	11	0
Adjective form (Pred>Attr)	55	17
Genitive before postposition	68	24
Nominative rel number agree	118	92
Numeral agreement	145	111

Table 3: Regression test results (for comparison)

in *BOUNDCORPUS*, which are based on good regression test results and knowledge about high frequency of the errors from experience as a manual proof reader. These error types are: adverbial use of the modal verb in third person singular, *soajttá* 'maybe s/he does'; use of attributive adjective forms instead of predicative forms; lexical confusion of the verbs *oahpásmuvvat>oahpástuvvat*; and reflexive pronoun errors. After fine-tuning the existing error mark-up on a bigger corpus that includes more fiction texts, and therefore other error types (*FREECORPUS*), we evaluated the well-performing rules on both *BOUNDCORPUS* and *FREECORPUS*, cf. Table 4.

Copula errors are by far the most frequent ones. In both corpora together, we found as many as 498 copula errors, four times as much as only in *BOUNDCORPUS*. All error types except for two have a precision above 85%. The low precision of reflexive and attributive > predicative adjective form confusion is not as low as it seems. In both cases, false positives are due to other errors in the text which lead to wrong corrections, but not detection. *GramDivvun* finds the error in the sentence, but fails to correct the error in the whole sentence structure based on other errors.

Altogether these are six general error types that have been released with functionalities in the first version of the Lule Sámi grammar checker.

Many of the rule types involve several rules. For example, copula correction includes three different rules: one for correcting from sentence initial to correct sentence internal forms, one for correct-

	Prec	Recall	# Err
Copula forms	92.77%	79.25%	498
Ine Rel agree	100.00%	71.43%	7
soajttá as Adv	91.67%	100.00%	11
Refl agree	50.00%	40.00%	10
oahpásmuvvat	85.71%	85.71%	7
Attr > Pred	50.00%	53.84%	13

Table 4: Evaluation on *FREECORPUS* and *BOUNDCORPUS*

ing the sentence internal form to the correct sentence initial form and one for choosing between the sentence internal forms *la* and *l*.

The benefit of our work has been twofold, we have improved both our tools and our marked-up data. Firstly, we have used rule development for automatic grammatical error detection, and secondly, we have improved grammatical error markup after running the grammar checker. This shows that consistency in manual error mark-up can be assisted by automatic grammar checking.

The evaluation shows despite good precision for the six rule types that were released, there are a number of false alarms and cases where *GramDivvun* does not find the error.

In ex. (8) and (9), the sentences are more complex than what we thought of when writing rules. In ex. (8) the grammar checker erroneously changes the attributive adjective *buosjes* 'tough' to predicative *buossje*. In this example there are two attributive adjectives connected with the conjunction *ja* meaning 'and'. Adding coordination conditions to the rules is fairly simple to fix.

(8) Adrian Nystø Mikkelsen gut aj la
Name who also is
buosjes ja vissjalis
tough.ADJ.ATTR and eager.ADJ.ATTR
bállotjiektje.
soccerplayer
'Adrian Nystø Mikkelsen who is a tough and eager soccer player.'

Another false alarm appears in ex. (9) where the subject is dropped and the grammar checker erroneously corrects the verb *vuojnáv* into 3.Pl since the 1.Sg pronoun *mån* 'I' is dropped.

(9) Hådjånav gå **vuojnáv** mijá
get upset.PRES.1SG when see.PRES.1SG our
galba biejsteduvvi.
signs destroy.PASSIVE.PRES.3PL
'I get upset when I see our signs being destroyed.'

Some of false alarms are due to combinations of errors. In ex. (10), *GramDivvun* erroneously changes the plural relative pronoun *ma* 'that' to singular *mij*. Therefore the subject is singular and the verb *guosski* 'regard' is also corrected by the grammar checker. Here *GramDivvun* changes *ma* to singular which is a false positive because of a wrong referent. Consequently it also tries to change the verb *guosski* to singular to correct the agreement with the relative pronoun.

(10) Lav válljim teoritevstajt
have.PRES.1SG choose.pst.ptcp text.PL.ACC
kompendijis **ma** **guosski**
compendium that.PL.NOM regard.PRES.3PL
álggoálmmukmetodologijav.
indigenous.methodology.ILL
'I have chosen texts from the compendium that regard indigenous methodology.'

We also have similar examples where the erroneous correction by the grammar checker is due to a combination of errors, but here it is the writer who has made two different errors. In ex. (11) the grammar checker corrects the attributive adjective *vâges* 'reliable' to singular *váhke*, where it should have been corrected to plural *váge*. The writer has made two errors, one of which is a number error in the verb *viertti* 'must' (present 3.Sg) which should be present 3.Pl *vierttiji*. *GramDivvun* misses this subject-verb agreement error and therefore the adjective attribute form is corrected to predicative singular form. Adding an agreement error rule to *GramDivvun* will lead to a correction of the second error.

(11) Moralla subttsasin de máhttá liehket
moral story then might be
rádna ***viertti** liehket
friend.PL.NOM must.PRES.2SG be
***váges** nubbe nuppijn jus
honest.ADJ.ATTR each other if
rádnastallam galggá bissot.
friendship will remain.
'The moral of the story might be that friends need to be honest with each other if the friendship is to remain.'

The same problem with a combination of errors happens in ex. (12), where the writer has misspelled the indefinite pronoun *iehtjádijn* 'with another'. Because of the typo the grammar checker erroneously corrects *oahpástuvvat* 'get to know' to *oahpásmuvvat*.

(12) Ietja dahki majt hálidi, ja
self do.PRES.3PL what want.PRES.3PL, and
dan båttå máhtá buorebut
that moment can.PRES.2SG better
*ietjadijn **oahpástuvvat**, javllá Inga Lill.
non.word get.to.know.INF, says Inga Lill
'Everyone does what they want, and at the same time you can get to know someone better, says Inga Lill.'

There are also examples where the rules of the grammar checker work fine, but where the grammar checker erroneously corrects because of problems with disambiguating homonymies. In ex. (13) the disambiguator construes *jage* 'year' to be nominative plural, when it actually is genitive singular. Because of the grammar checker construes *jage* to be the subject of the sentence it corrects the sentence-initial present copula form *le* 'is' to the 3Pl form *li* instead of the correct 3Sg form *la*.

(13) Badjel guoktalåk jage
Over twenty years
***le** duodje
be.PRES.3SG.SENT.INIT Sámi.handcraft
munji årrum vájmoássjen ja oasse iehtjam
me be heart.case and part my
identitehtas.
identity.
'For over twenty years Sámi handcraft has been close to my heart and a part of my identity.'

The evaluation shows that even though the grammar checker works well with six rules, there are still complex issues that cause the grammar checker to fail even for these types of errors. More errors in the same sentence makes it harder for the grammar checker. It is therefore important that the users know that this grammar checker is predominantly meant for L1 users and that upon its release, it does not work very well for second language learners' texts, yet. The evaluation shows that building a grammar checker for L1 users before L2 users is a good way to go, as the tool performs better with only one error in the sentence, and proficiency writers are assumed to make less errors.

6 Conclusion and future plans

We have released a tool for grammatical detection and correction of Lule Sámi (*GramDivvun*) to support the Lule Sámi language community in writing. We evaluated our tool and based on the evaluation, we chose six general error types that met our quality requirements and were ready to be released. These are corrections regarding copula forms, lexical confusion of *oahpásmuvvat-oahpástuvvat*, number agreement for reflexive pronouns, the use of the modal verb *soajttá* as an adverb, confusion of attributive and predicative adjective forms, and finally number agreement of inessive relative pronoun forms. While our evaluation corpus is still a bit too small to have a good representation of all errors, it was evident that copula errors are very frequent, and the other error types were also represented. Copula errors also show the best precision with 96% and recall of 84%. In other error types, we rely on our manual proof-reading experience to know about their frequency. This goes hand in hand with our wish to focus on user demands. In the future we will improve precision and recall for the correction of existing error types by testing on more syntactic contexts. This means we will we need to enhance the corpora with error mark-up. In addition we will improve the quality of error rules that have not been included in this version of *GramDivvun* with the goal of releasing them. We can also conclude that even L1 language users typically make several errors in a sentence. This is due to low literacy in Lule Sámi, and interference errors caused by bilingualism. Our focus must therefore be a tool that can handle these types of sentences.

References

Kenneth R Beesley and Lauri Karttunen. 2003. Finite-state morphology: Xerox tools and techniques. *CSLI, Stanford.*

Eckhard Bick and Tino Didriksen. 2015. CG-3 – beyond classical Constraint Grammar. In *Proceedings of the 20th Nordic Conference of Computational Linguistics (NoDaLiDa 2015)*, pages 31–39. Linköping University Electronic Press, Linköpings universitet.

Inger Johansen. 2006. det er ikkje eit museumsspråk – det har noko med framtida å gjera ei sosiolingvistisk undersøking av revitaliseringa av sørsamisk. Master's thesis, Institutt for nordistikk og litteraturvitskap, NTNU.

Fred Karlsson. 1990. Constraint Grammar as a Framework for Parsing Running Text. In *Proceedings of the 13th Conference on Computational Linguistics (COLING 1990)*, volume 3, pages 168–173,

Helsinki, Finland. Association for Computational Linguistics.

Fred Karlsson, Atro Voutilainen, Juha Heikkilä, and Arto Anttila. 1995. *Constraint Grammar: A Language-Independent System for Parsing Unrestricted Text.* Mouton de Gruyter, Berlin.

Susanna Angéus Kuoljok. 1997. *Nominalavledningar på ahka i lulesamiskan.* Acta Universitatis Upsaliensis.

Susanna Angéus Kuoljok. 2002. Julevsámegiella. *Bårjås: Julevsámegiella uddni - ja idet?*, pages 10–18.

Dale McCreery. 2006. http://www.malsmb.ca/docs/challenges-and-solutions-in-adult-cree-learning.pdf Challenges and solutions in adult acquisition of cree as a second language. Master's thesis, BA, Canadian University College.

Inga Lill Sigga Mikkelsen, Linda Wiechetek, and Flammie A Pirinen. 2022. https://doi.org/10.18653/v1/2022.computel-1.19 Reusing a multi-lingual setup to bootstrap a grammar checker for a very low resource language without data. In *Proceedings of the Fifth Workshop on the Use of Computational Methods in the Study of Endangered Languages*, pages 149–158, Dublin, Ireland. Association for Computational Linguistics.

Christopher Moseley. 2010. www.unesco.org/culture/en/endangeredlanguages/atlas *Atlas of the World's Languages in Danger*, volume 3. UNESCO.

Sjur N. Moshagen, Tommi A. Pirinen, and Trond Trosterud. 2013. Building an open-source development infrastructure for language technology projects. In *NODALIDA*.

Tommi A. Pirinen and Krister Lindén. 2014. State-of-the-art in weighted finite-state spell-checking. In *Proceedings of the 15th International Conference on Computational Linguistics and Intelligent Text Processing - Volume 8404*, CICLing 2014, pages 519–532, Berlin, Heidelberg. Springer-Verlag.

Håkan Rydving. 2013. *Words and varieties : lexical variation in Saami.* Société Finno-Ougrienne.

Pekka Sammallahti. 1998. *The Saami Languages: an introduction.* Davvi girji.

SIKOR. UiT The Arctic University of Norway and the Norwegian Saami Parliament's Saami text collection, Version 06.11.2018. `http://gtweb.uit.no/korp`. Accessed: 2018-11-06.

Nils Eric Spiik. 1989. *Lulesamisk grammatik.* Sameskolstyrelsen.

Mikael Svonni. 2008. Språksituationen för samerna i sverige. *Samiskan i Sverige, rapport från språkkampanjerådet*, pages 22–35.

Trond Trosterud. 2021. Utan tastatur, ingen tekst: om det språkteknologiske grunnlaget for språka våre. In Karin Kvarfordt Niia, editor, *Framgång för små språk.*, pages 68–73. Små språk i Norden.

Linda Wiechetek, Katri Hiovain-Asikainen, Inga Lill Sigga Mikkelsen, Sjur Moshagen, Flammie Pirinen, Trond Trosterud, and Børre Gaup. 2022. https://aclanthology.org/2022.lrec-1.125 Unmasking the myth of effortless big data - making an open source multi-lingual infrastructure and building language resources from scratch. In *Proceedings of the Thirteenth Language Resources and Evaluation Conference*, pages 1167–1177, Marseille, France. European Language Resources Association.

Linda Wiechetek, Sjur Nørstebø Moshagen, Børre Gaup, and Thomas Omma. 2019. Many shades of grammar checking – launching a constraint grammar tool for North Sámi. In *Proceedings of the NoDaLiDa 2019 Workshop on Constraint Grammar - Methods, Tools and Applications*, NEALT Proceedings Series 33:8, pages 35–44.

Linda Wiechetek, Flammie A Pirinen, Børre Gaup, and Thomas Omma. 2021. https://aclanthology.org/2021.iwclul-1.6 No more fumbling in the dark - quality assurance of high-level NLP tools in a multi-lingual infrastructure. In *Proceedings of the Seventh International Workshop on Computational Linguistics of Uralic Languages*, pages 47–56, Syktyvkar, Russia (Online). Association for Computational Linguistics.

Jussi Ylikoski. 2022. Lule Saami. *The Oxford Guide to the Uralic Languages*, pages 130–146.

A South Sámi Grammar Checker for Stopping Language Change

Linda Wiechetek
UiT Norgga árktalaš universitehta
linda.wiechetek@uit.no

Maja Lisa Kappfjell
UiT Norgga árktalaš universitehta
maja.l.kappfjell@uit.no

Abstract

We have released and evaluated the first South Sámi grammar checker *GramDivvun*. It corrects two frequent error types that are caused by and causing language change and a loss of the language's morphological richness. These general error types comprise a number of errors regarding the adjective paradigm (confusion of attributive and predicative forms) and the negation paradigm. In addition, our work includes a classification of common error types regarding the adjective and negation paradigms and lead to extensive grammatical error mark-up of our gold corpus. We achieve precisions above 71% for both adjective and negation error correction.

1 Introduction

Language change is a natural process caused by various factors in all languages. Indigenous languages are in a special situation, as they typically need to compete with a majority language, which is used by the bilingual language user more often and in more domains. South Sámi is in a critical situation that requires concrete measures so that morphological richness is taught to the next generation and does not get lost. While we do not think we can stop language change altogether, we do think that we can provide necessary grammatical support for South Sámi writers when other help is not available. A language community that wants to preserve certain language structures, will only be able to so if someone can give feedback to language learners, both L1 and L2.

The school system does not provide sufficient language support for the South Sámi language. Students have only a few hours a week to learn the language. The teachers of South Sámi have to select what they teach, which are typically the topics that are satisfactorily described in the grammar books, such as the verbal and nominal paradigms. Other topics, such as the adjective and negation paradigms, on the other hand, are described very superficially and lack information about the variation in the spoken language. A grammar checker that corrects grammatical errors of the latter types can deliver feedback and thereby improve grammatical knowledge in these areas.

In this article, we focus on two very frequent grammatical error types of morphological forms that the language community wishes to preserve, which has been expressed in professional meetings of teachers and translators. Some of these tendencies have been decided on by the Sámi normative institution.[1] Those include adjective inflection and inflection of verbal periphrastic negation. An investigation in 2018 (Kappfjell and Trosterud, forthcoming) showed tendencies of adjective classes being reduced from four to two classes. Blokland and Inaba (2015) cover negation in South Sámi and shows that at least four non-traditional paradigms of past tense copula negation are used in contemporary text. There are strong tendencies in the language community itself to preserve the traditional paradigm as it is presented in the written grammar. (Bergsland, 1994)

The first South Sámi gammar checker, *GramDivvun*, has been released 31st May 2023 and is freely available for MS Word and GoogleDocs.[2] We encourage the use of our proofing tools in schools and other educational institutions, publishing houses and the Sámi government.

[1] https://sametinget.no/sprak/sami-giellagaldu/?sprak=14
[2] https://divvun.no/en/korrektur/gramcheck.html

Proceedings of the NoDaLiDa 2023 Workshop on Constraint Grammar - Methods, Tools and Applications, pages 46–54

2 Background

2.1 Language situation

According to Blokland and Hasselblatt (2003, p.110), there are about 2,000 ethnic South Sámi, of which approximately 300-500 are South Sámi speakers. There are two major varieties in South Sámi: northern (or Asele) South Sámi and South (or Jamtland) South Sámi (Sammallahti, 1998, p.24), but the differences between the two are minor, and limited mostly to phonetics and morphology. South Sámi has a written standard, which is adhered to especially (children's) published fiction. South Sámi is an official language in altogether four communities in Norway: Aarborte (Norwegian: Hattfjelldal), Snåase, (Norwegian: Snåsa), Raarvihke (Norwegian: Røyrvik) and Plaassja (Norwegian: Røros) in Norway. In Sweden there are 10 South Sámi communities; Bïerje (Swedish: Berg), Kraapohke (Swedish: Dorotea), Herjedaelie (Swedish: Swedish: Härjedalen), Krokome (Swedish: Krokom), Luspie (Swedish: Storuman), Straejmie (Swedish: Strömsund), Upmeje (Swedish: Umeå), Vualtjere (Vilhelmina), Älvdaelie (Swedish: Älvdalen) and Åare (Swedish: Åre). There are some minor differences between the orthographies used in Sweden and Norway, e.g. the letter *ä* is used in Sweden where the letter *æ* is used in Norway.

There is a lack of standardization and clarification regarding grammatical variants that are due to language change and simplification. Adjectives and negation paradigms, which we will deal with in this article, are exemplary cases of these changes.

2.2 Technical background

The technological implementation of the grammar checker is based on rule-based natural language processing: finite-state automata (*FST*) for morphological analysis (Beesley and Karttunen, 2003; Lindén et al., 2013; Pirinen and Lindén, 2014) and constraint grammar (Karlsson, 1990; Didriksen, 2010) for syntactic and semantic as well as other sentence-level processing. In our work, we use the free open source implementation VISLCG-3 (Bick and Didriksen, 2015). The South Sámi tools are publicly available[3]. It is part of a (multilingual infrastructure (Moshagen et al., 2013) *https://github.com/giellaltGiellaLT*), which includes 130 languages.

GramDivvun first analyzes the morphological structure of a text together with part-of-speech tagging, and displays all homonymy of a given form. In addition lexical semantic tags are added to (especially) nouns. A number Constraint Grammar modules are then used for ambiguous tokenisation of compounds, ordinals and abbreviations, morpho-syntactic disambiguation of word form homonymy, valency additions and lastly error detection and correction. Error detection and correction is accomplished by means of a set of hand-written rules that first identify an erroneous form in a given morpho-syntactic context, labels it, and then exchanges an incorrect tag combination with another one, which then is used to generate the correct form. The full modular structure is described in Wiechetek (2019). As Figure 1 shows, *GramDivvun* is realized in the right-hand column and gives feedback and suggestions for South Sámi errors as in this case the negation form *Ean*.

Our work started out with collecting error sentences according to error type. Those sentences were used to develop rules for *GramDivvun* and typically contain between 10 and 70 examples that are relevant to a certain error type. These regression tests are used for developing and quality ensuring our tool, cf. Wiechetek et al. (2021). Regression testing shows that error correction for both negation and adjective forms look promising with precisons of up to 80% when starting our work.

2.3 Motivation

A recent survey shows that language technology is used to a far greater extent by minority languages and indigenous languages than by state-bearing majority languages such as Norwegian. (Trosterud, 2019) The size of the language community also plays a role: South Sámi use language technology aids to a far greater extent than North Sámi. Language technology tools are therefore central to the revitalization of South Sámi, and our goal is to be able to provide good tools to the South Sámi language community. One of the authors is a member of the South Sámi language community that serves as a reference for linguistic questions regarding grammar and the lexicon. Competent speakers with clear language intuitions are essential for a language community. South Sámi school

[3]https://github.com/giellalt/lang-sma/

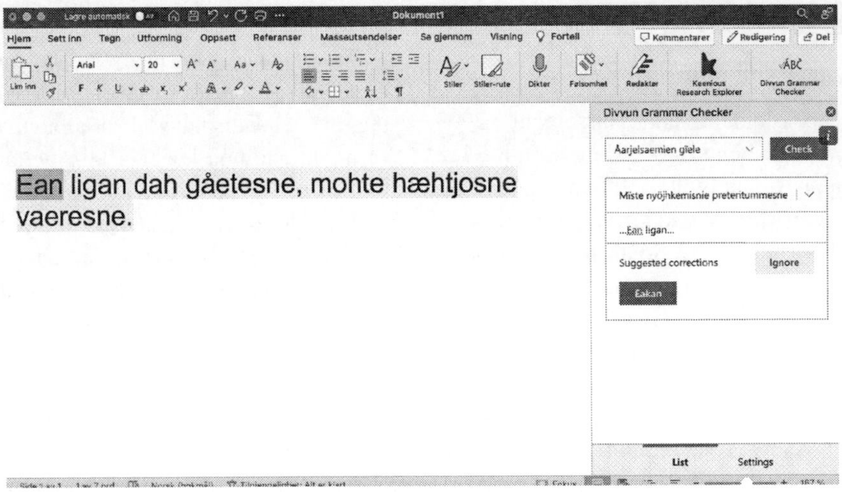

Figure 1: *GramDivvun* integrated in MS Word

children of the 80s who were taught by Anna Jacobsen,(Jacobsen, 2013) (teacher in Hattfjelldal) and Ella Holm Bull (teacher in Snåsa) had a strong grammarian with clear expectations of how correct language should be as guidance.(Kappfjell, 2014) When language experts from the past generation pass away, the bearers of this knowledge disappear. In a reality where South Sámi is not used as frequently in daily life as it used to be, we need other tools to ensure that feedback for correct and incorrect language is available. Otherwise, there is a lot of insecurity about it and instead of using the language, people keep quiet and do not dare to write.

3 The South Sámi grammar checker

3.1 Adjective errors

South Sámi grammars that write about the adjective system often state that the adjective paradigm is unclear. In the dictionaries and in the text corpora, there is a lot of variation.

According to earlier grammarians, two-syllable adjectives usually have two forms in the positive, one of them ending in a vowel and the other of them ending in *-s*.

These two forms can be attributive or predicative forms. Alternatively, there can be only one form for both attributive and predicative. According to earlier grammarians, the comparative forms are built on the predicative form. However, in today's South Sámi there are also comparatives built on attributive forms. Table 1 shows all four attribute-predicative combinations are those according to these grammars (Lagercrantz, 1926; Bergsland, 1946; Hasselbrink, 1981-1985; Magga and Mattsson Magga, 2012).

Attributive	**Predicative**
vowel (*buerie*)	vowel (*buerie*)
vowel (*skïemtje*)	-s (*skïemtjes*)
-s (*vihkeles*)	vowel (*vihkele*)
-s (*båeries*)	-s (*båeries*)

Table 1: Adjective paradigms in positive

In addition to that, some of the adjective forms can also be adverbs. The predicative form *vihkele* 'important' for example is homonymous to the adverbial form. Other adjectives have more part-of-speech homonymies. *buerie* 'good' is for example both attributive and predicative form of an adjective, but can at the same time also be a noun. The form *båetije* 'coming' is both an adjective, deverbal noun and a present participle of a verb.

Kappfjell and Trosterud (forthcoming) show that text collections of modern South Sámi exhibit others tendencies of adjectives inflection than its mentioned on the earlier grammars. They come to the conclusion that modern South Sámi shows the same system as before, but the attribute is more frequent than a predicative: 60% vs. 30%. The other tendency is that instead of four adjective classes, there are only two of them where attributive and predicative are homonymous, either ending in a vowel or in -s. The investigation shows, that predicative and attribute forms are the same in 98.4% of the cases. Only 8.7% of the adjective types display variation. This system appears to be very stable and consistent. However, there is a desire in the language community to revert the system and go back to and teach morphological richness to new generations, as the author of this paper can confirm.

We have to keep in mind that South Sámi language orthography was approved in 1978, and there has been a careful revitalization at the Sámi schools in Snåsa and Hattfjelldal at the Norwegian side of South Sámi area. There are approximately 500 speakers, but only 1/10 actually write the language as well. South Sámi training has been deficient in that it has been cut short to only a few hours, and the teachers have thus not been given the space they have needed to be able to provide complete training in the most important grammatical systems.

(1) Saemien kultuvre lea **gånkaladtje** jïh *__**tjaebpies**__.
Sámi culture is royal.PRED and beautiful.ATTR
'The Sámi culture is royal and beautiful.'

For a rule-based grammar checker this means that we need to distinguish between adjectives that have one form for both attributive and predicative forms and those that differ in their forms. We resolve this by adding an early rule to the syntactic analyzer module preceding the grammar checking rules. The rule below adds a secondary tag <AttrPred> to each adjective with both an attributive (Attr) reading and a predicative reading in the same cohort. Since this rule precedes all disambiguation rules, both readings are still available, and the tag ensures that this information is kept throughout the analysis.

```
SUBSTITUTE (A) (A <AttrPred>)
TARGET A
IF (0 Attr LINK 0 (A Nom));
```

The error detection rules are ADD-rules. They add an error tag, here *&msyn-adj-attr-pred* to the erroneous form in a syntactic context. There are different syntactic contexts that require different types of rules. The one below pays attention to a nominative subject to its left and a possible copula between the adjective and the copula. Since copulas can be dropped in South Sámi, the subject can be an important marker. In addition it excludes a noun to its right.

```
ADD (&msyn-adj-attr-pred)
TARGET (A Attr) IF
(*-1 Nom
BARRIER (*) - REALCOPULAS - Ela)
(NEGATE 0 ATTR-PRED-A
OR A + Sg + Nom OR A-ATTR-ONLY)
(NOT 1 N) ;
```

The second context below is a visible copula that can be either by itself or together with a negation verb. If the subject is dropped, the copula is the decisive marker for predicative forms. Again we do not want a noun to the right of the adjective. This rule explicitly asks for an end of sentence after the adjective form.

```
ADD (&msyn-adj-attr-pred)
TARGET (A Attr) IF
(NEGATE 0 ATTR-PRED-A OR
A + Sg + Nom OR A-ATTR-ONLY)
(1 EOS)
(*-1 (Neg Ind) OR
REALCOPULAS BARRIER NOT-ADV-PCLE);
```

The third case is a coordination context where the predicative adjective is coordinated with another predicative adjective, which shows that the form should be predicative rather than attributive.

```
ADD (&msyn-adj-attr-pred)
TARGET (A Attr) IF

(-1 CC LINK *-1 Nom
BARRIER (*) - REALCOPULAS)
(NEGATE 0 ATTR-PRED-A
OR A + Sg + Nom OR A-ATTR-ONLY)
(NOT 1 N);
```

3.2 Negation errors

Standard negation in South Sámi utilizes a negative auxiliary and a connegative form of the lexical verb. The basic paradigm usually presented in grammars, cf. Bergsland (1946, pp.169–170), Hasselbrink (1981-1985, p.145), Magga and Mattsson Magga (2012, p.38), is one where the negative auxiliary has two moods (indicative and imperative) and two simple tenses (present and past tense) The connegative form ends in -h and is homonymous with the second person singular of the imperative. Depending on inflection type, it may also be identical to the second person singular or the third person plural of the present indicative. (Blokland and Inaba, 2015)

But according to Blokland and Inaba (2015), in different (Southern vs. Northern) dialects there are diverging inflectional patterns for negation, some of which are not according to the norm. Four of those are constructions regarding the past tense of the negation auxiliary *ij* together with the connegative verb form *leah* 'be'.

Table 2 shows the typical errors which are in South Sámi texts. In Table 2, Blokland describes the variants of Table 2 as variants which are in use in the Northern South Sámi area. We have one rules to correct the errors in Table 2, one for the negation verb *ij* making it agree with the person and number of the subject instead of treating it as an uninflected adverb (just as in Norwegian, where negation is an adverb like in English).

Error	Correct	Translation
∗**ij** lim	im lim	'I was not'
ih lih	ih lih	'you were not'
ij lij	ij lij	's/he was not'
∗**ij** limen	ean limen	'we two were not'
∗**ij** liden	idien liden	'you two were not'
∗**ij** ligan	eakan ligan	'they two were not'
∗**ij** limh	ibie limh	'we were not'
∗**ij** lidh	idie lidh	'you were not'
∗**ij** lin	eah lin	'they were not'

Table 2: Paradigm for erroneous negation constructions (type 1 - past tense)

The error type in Table 3 is corrected for the connegative past tense form *lih* - only past tense connegative forms of the copula (not any other main verb) - should agree with the negation verb. However, as a common error, the copula connegative form *lih*, which is second person singular and ends in *-h* is used for the whole paradigm. The rule *msyn-NegPrt-lih-congruence* corrects this error type.

Error	Correct	Translation
im ***lih**	im lim	'I was not'
ih lih	ih lih	'you were not'
ij ***lih**	ij lij	's/he was not'

Table 3: Paradigm for erroneous negation constructions (type 2)

The negation in Table 4, is an older form of negation documented in Bergsland (1994), which is not included in the current norm. Since it is not very frequent in spoken and written South Sámi, we have not developed any rules for it yet. The connegative 3rd person form *leam* is used instead of *lij*. This form is now only analyzed as the first person singular present tense. It would be interesting to investigate if the past tense use is related to the North Sámi *lean* past tense connegative of *leat* 'to be'.

Typical error 3	Correct	Translation
im lim	im lim	'I was not'
ih lih	ih lih	'you were not'
ij ***leam**	ij **lij**	's/he was not'

Table 4: Paradigm for erroneous negation constructions (type 3)

Bergsland (1994) describes the variants in Table 5 as Southern variants. Even though this negation system is not so frequently used in the South Sámi text collection, it is frequent in oral speech, as reported by one of the authors, who is herself a member of the South Sámi language community. We therefore expect this error type to become more frequent in writing in the future with increasing South Sámi publications. The negation verb in this error type follows the paradigm for main verbs (as opposed to the paradigm for copulas). That means it uses the form *idtjim/eedtjem* (which is used as a negation verb with main verbs) instead of *im* (which is used for copulas). The connegative form of the past tense copula on the other hand is not inflected (as it is done with main verbs) while it should agree in person and number with the negation verb. This error type is dealt with by two rules in *GramDivvun*, one for the negation verb and the other one for the connegative form.

(2) Mohte ***eakan** ***edtjigan**
but NEG.PRES.3DU be.PRED.3DU
juakadidh.
separate
'They should not seperate.'

In habitive constructions expressing possession, there is a form of *lea* 'to be' agreeing with the possessed item in number and person, and the possessor in genitive case. Typical errors regard the agreement between the copula and the possessed item as in ex. (3), where 3.Sg *ij* 'is' should be 3.Pl because of plural *måvhkah* 'trousers'. This agreement error is corrected by a separate rule since it typically appears in habitive construction.

Error	Correct	Translation
∗**eedtjem lih**	im lim	'I was not'
∗**eedtjh lih**	ih lih	'you were not'
∗**eedtji lih**	ij lij	's/he was not'
∗**eedtjemen/** ∗**eedtjien lih**	ean limen	'we two were not'
∗**eedtjeden lih**	idien liden	'you two were not'
∗**eedtjeben lih**	eakan ligan	'they two were not'
∗**eedtjuvh lih**	ibie limh	'we were not'
∗**eedtjede lih**	idie lidh	'you were not'
∗**eedtjen/** ∗**eedtjies lih**	eah lin	'they were not'

Table 5: Paradigm for erroneous negation constructions (type 4)

(3) *****ij** leah dov
NEG.PRES.3SG be.CONNEG you.GEN
naan rööpses måvhkah
some/red trouser.NOM.PL
'You do not have any red trousers.'

One error type regards the negation verb itself. In past tense it should be in congruence with the subsequent past tense connegative form. In example (4), the form *ean* (1.Du) should actually be *eakan* (3.Du) as in ex. (5) as the connegative form *ligan* is a third person dual.

(4) ***Ean** ligan dah gåetesne,
NEG.1DU be.PAST.3DU this home.INE.SG
mohte hæhtjosne vaeresne.
this cabin.INE.SG mountain.INE.SG
'They were not at home, but in the cabin in the mountain'

(5) **Eakan** ligan dah gåetesne, mohte hæhtjosne vaeresne.
NEG.3DU be.PAST.3DU this home.INE.SG this cabin.INE.SG mountain.INE.SG
'They were not at home, but in the cabin in the mountain'

GramDivvun detects the error by means of an *ADD*-rule that adds a label to a past tense negation form (*Prt ConNeg*) if the negation verb to the left of it agrees in number and person with it. Each *ADD*-rule pairs with one or several *COPY*-rules, which pick up on the error tag, copy the morphological tag and lemma combination that makes out a form, and exchange the unwanted tags with the desired ones. The *COPY*-rule below exchanges second or third person singular with first person singular. The second *COPY*-rule exchanges first or third person singular with second person singular.

```
ADD (&msyn-ConNegPrt-congruence)
TARGET (Prt ConNeg) + $$SG-PERS IF
(-1 ("ij" Prs Neg) - $$SG-PERS) ;


COPY (Sg1 &SUGGEST) EXCEPT
(Sg2 &msyn-ConNegPrt-congruence)
OR (Sg3 &msyn-ConNegPrt-congruence)
TARGET (&msyn-ConNegPrt-congruence)
IF (-1 Sg1);

COPY (Sg2 &SUGGEST) EXCEPT
(Sg1 &msyn-ConNegPrt-congruence)
OR (Sg3 &msyn-ConNegPrt-congruence)
TARGET (&msyn-ConNegPrt-congruence)
IF (-1 Sg2);
```

A second typical error is the use of the third person singular form of the negation verb *ij* as a default, as in example (6). Here the first person dual form of the connegative form *limen* shows the actual person and number of the verb phrase, and the negation verb should agree with it, i.e. *ij* should be changed to *ean* (1.Du).

(6) ***Ij** limen månnoeh
NEG.3SG be.CONNEG.PAST.1DU there
desnie.

'We were not there.'

```
ADD (&msyn-Neg-VFinitt-ConNeg)
TARGET (Ind Prs) + $$ALL-PERS
OR (Ind Prt) + $$ALL-PERS
(-1 ("ij" Prs Neg) + $$ALL-PERS)
(NEGATE 0 ConNeg) ;
```

A third type changes a finite verb form to a connegative verb form, cf. ex. (7). Here, *edtjigan* should be changed to *edtjh*, and subsequently the tense of the negation verb *eakan* should be changed to past tense as marked by the connegative, i.e. *idtjigan*.

(7) Mohte **eakan** edtjigan
But NEG.PRS.3DU will.PAST.3DU
juakadidh.
separate
'But they would not separate.'

4 Evaluation

The evaluation is based on a part of *SIKOR*, the South Sámi corpus,(sik) containing administrative, law, religious, non-fiction, fiction, and science texts. The evaluation corpus is marked up for the following error types - spelling errors, morpho-syntactic errors, syntactic errors, formatting errors, real word errors, etc. It consists of a publicly available corpus, *FREECORPUS* (34,512 words) and a part that is restricted by copyright *BOUNDCORPUS* (166,483 words). For evaluation purposes we use the marked-up parts of them, hence *FREECORPUS* and *BOUNDCORPUS*.

The results of the evaluation are shown in Table 6. The quality is measured using basic precision and recall, such that recall $R = \frac{t_p}{t_p + f_n}$ and precision $P = \frac{t_p}{t_p + f_p}$, where t_p is a count of true positives, f_p false positives, t_n true negatives and f_n false negatives.

Adjective rules include both way confusions between attributive and predicative singular/plural form (attr>pred, attr>pred.pl) and pred>attr), a confusion between attributive forms and adverb derivations (attr>adv). Negation rules include (tense and person) errors of the negation verb and errors of the connegative form. The latter can be finite forms or infinitives. Errors can also be application of the main verb paradigm (connegative ending in -h) for the copula paradigm. While the main verb connegative form does not inflect for person and tense, the copula paradigm inflects for person and tense.

Precision for adjective and negation errors are both above 71%. Recall is above 79%. We expect precision to raise to close to 90% after fine-tuning the rules and fixing the last issues of corpus mark-up. The corpus shows that both error types are frequent (188 and 68 errors respectively) and their correction is relevant for the language community. All rules have been released May 31st 2023 and are freely available for the South Sámi language community. It needs to be marked-up for grammatical errors of the type we are investigating. Previous versions did not include certain types of mark-up for the following reasons: 1) The norm had not beeb clear at that point of time. 2) Manual mark-up is cumbersome, and not all error instances are easy to detect.

When further investigating the reasons for the shortcomings of our tool we found the following: In ex. (8) attributive *guelhties* is erroneously corrected to predicative *guelhtie*. The reason for that is that rules are missing a condition for possible coordination. This can easily be specified and corrected.

	Precision	**Recall**	**# Err**
Adjective errors	71.81%	85.99%	188
Negation errors	75.00%	79.69%	68

Table 6: Evaluation of the South Sámi grammar checker on *FREECORPUS*

(8) Bovtside leah **guelhties** jih
reindeer.ILL be.3SG cool.ATTR and
gaaloes giesie hijven.
rainy.cool.ATTR summer good.PRED
'For the reindeer, a cool and rainy summer is good.'

In ex. (9) there is another false positive. Even though the adjective *aelhkie* 'simple' precedes a noun, it is not attributive. Instead, it is part of an infinitive construction of the type 'it is easy to + infinitive'. Therefore the adjective should have the predicate form. However, being an SOV language, in South Sámi, the infinitive can be preceded by an object, here *ditnie-laejkiem* 'tin wire', which leads to the adjective being adjacent to the noun, a typical attributive context.

(9) Ij leah **aelhkie**
be.3SG be.CONNEG easy.PRED
ditnielaejkiem giesedh.
tin.wire.ACC pull.INF
'it is not easy to pull a tin wire.'

The previous example is a recurrent false positive type, just as in ex. (10), where predicative *vihkele* 'important' is erroneously corrected to attributive *vihkeles* since it is followed by a noun. However, this is an infinitive construction with an object before the infinitive just as in the previous example, and the predicative form of the adjective is correct.

(10) lea **vihkele** saemiengïelem
be.3SG important.PRED Sámi language.ACC
åtnose bertedh bievnese- jïh
use.ILL adjust information and
gaskesadteme teknologijisnie
communication technology.ACC
'it is important to adjust the Sámi language for use in information and communication technology'

Another false positive caused by homonymy, in this case between adjective and verb, is the mark-up of the present participle form *båetije* 'coming' as in ex. (11).

(11) ***båetije** saemien *siebredahken
come.PRES.PTC Sámi.GEN society.GEN
dïejveldimmine
discussion.INE
'in future debates about the Sámi society'

All three syntactic contexts can easily be included in error correction rules as exceptions.

As there are many more negation error types, negation rule shortcomings are the following. One issue negation rules have not been paying attention to is the homonymy between finite and a connegative forms like *lij* 's/he was' in ex. (12), resulting in a false positive. *GramDivvun* tries to correct the form based on the assumption that it is a finite form. However, a negative condition excluding possible connegatives, should take care of this problem.

(12) Saemien *siebredahken tseegkemisnie
Sámi.GEN society.GEN building.INE,
ij **lij** gaajhkide
NEG.PAST.3SG be.PAST.CONNEG all.ILL
saemientjïertide seamma nuepie
Sámi.groups.ILL same possibility
'In building the Sámi society, there were not the same opportunities for all Sámi groups'

5 Conclusion

In this article we present the first South Sámi grammar checker for adjective and negation error correction, which are both very frequent error types in contemporary writing and speech. Our evaluation on an error marked-up corpus confirms these tendencies. The loss of language arenas in a bilingual society and insufficient grammar teaching in schools have contributed to interference errors and a loss of morphological distinctions. One of the consequences is the use of a simplified adjective paradigm. The negation paradigm, on the other hand, displays a lot of variation in use, both regarding the negation verb and the connegative form. There are errors where the copula copies the main verb paradigm, others where the negation verb is used as an adverb, or agreement is neglected.

The grammar checker tool plays an important role in language revitalization as wished by the language community, implementing normative decisions by means of much needed grammatical feedback. *GramDivvun* shows precisions above 71% for adjective and negation form correction. *GramDivvun* for Microsoft Word and Google Docs has been released in May 2023 and is freely available for download. Future plans include improvement of existing error type correction and correction of other frequent error types.

References

SIKOR uit the arctic university of norway and the norwegian saami parliament's saami text collection, version 06.11.2018. `http://gtweb.uit.no/korp`. Accessed: 2018-11-06.

Kenneth R Beesley and Lauri Karttunen. 2003. Finite-state morphology: Xerox tools and techniques. *CSLI, Stanford*.

Knut Bergsland. 1946. *Røros-lappisk grammatikk: et forsøk på strukturell språkbeskrivelse / av Knut Bergsland*. H. Aschehoug Co. (W. Nygaard); Cambridge, Mass.: Harvard University Press, Oslo.

Knut Bergsland. 1994. *Sydsamisk Grammatikk*. Davvi Girji o.s., Karasjok. 1. utgave 1982.

Eckhard Bick and Tino Didriksen. 2015. CG-3 – beyond classical Constraint Grammar. In *Proceedings of the 20th Nordic Conference of Computational Linguistics (NoDaLiDa 2015)*, pages 31–39. Linköping University Electronic Press, Linköpings universitet.

Rogier Blokland and Cornelius Hasselblatt. 2003. *The endangered Uralic languages*. John Benjamins Publishing Company.

Rogier Blokland and Nobufumi Inaba. 2015. https://doi.org/10.1075/tsl.108.14blo *Negation in South Saami*, pages 377–398. Uppsala University University of Turku.

Tino Didriksen. 2010. http://visl.sdu.dk/cg3/vislcg3.pdf (Accessed 2017-11-29) *Constraint Grammar Manual: 3rd version of the CG formalism variant*. GrammarSoft ApS, Denmark.

Gustav Hasselbrink. 1981-1985. *Oårj'elsaamien baaguog'ärjaa, Skrifter utgivna genom Dialekt- och folkminnesarkivet i Uppsala Ser. C, Lapskt språk och lapsk kultur nr 4, Lundequistska bokhandeln*. Uppsala.

Anna Jacobsen. 2013. *Mijjen Gïele*. Sijti Jarnge, Hattfjelldal.

Lena Kappfjell. 2014. *Tjaalehvuekieh*. ČálliidLágádus, Kárášjohka-Karasjok.

Maja Kappfjell and Trond Trosterud. forthcoming. Åarjelsaemien gööktelïhtse adjektijvi gramatihke. page .

Fred Karlsson. 1990. Constraint grammar as a framework for parsing unrestricted text. In *Proceedings of the 13th International Conference of Computational Linguistics*, volume 3, pages 168–173, Helsinki.

Eliel Lagercrantz. 1926. *Sprachlehre des Westlappischen nach der Mundart von Arjeplog. Mémoires de la Société Finno-ougrienne LV.* Helsinki.

Krister Lindén, Erik Axelson, Senka Drobac, Sam Hardwick, Juha Kuokkala, Jyrki Niemi, Tommi A Pirinen, and Miikka Silfverberg. 2013. Hfst—a system for creating nlp tools. In *International workshop on systems and frameworks for computational morphology*, pages 53–71. Springer.

Ole Henrik Magga and Lajla Mattsson Magga. 2012. *Sørsamisk grammatikk.* Davvi girji, Kárásjohkka.

Sjur N. Moshagen, Tommi A. Pirinen, and Trond Trosterud. 2013. Building an open-source development infrastructure for language technology projects. In *NODALIDA*.

Tommi A. Pirinen and Krister Lindén. 2014. State-of-the-art in weighted finite-state spell-checking. In *Proceedings of the 15th International Conference on Computational Linguistics and Intelligent Text Processing - Volume 8404*, CICLing 2014, pages 519–532, Berlin, Heidelberg. Springer-Verlag.

Pekka Sammallahti. 1998. *The Saami Languages: An Introduction.* Davvi Girji, Karasjohka.

Trond Trosterud. 2019. Kva bruker vi minoritetsspråksordbøker til? ein studie av brukarloggane for tolv tospråklege ordbøker. *LexicoNordica*, pages 177–198.

Linda Wiechetek, Sjur Nørstebø Moshagen, Børre Gaup, and Thomas Omma. 2019. Many shades of grammar checking – launching a constraint grammar tool for North Sámi. In *Proceedings of the NoDaLiDa 2019 Workshop on Constraint Grammar - Methods, Tools and Applications*, NEALT Proceedings Series 33:8, pages 35–44.

Linda Wiechetek, Flammie A Pirinen, Børre Gaup, and Thomas Omma. 2021. https://aclanthology.org/2021.iwclul-1.6 No more fumbling in the dark - quality assurance of high-level NLP tools in a multi-lingual infrastructure. In *Proceedings of the Seventh International Workshop on Computational Linguistics of Uralic Languages*, pages 47–56, Syktyvkar, Russia (Online). Association for Computational Linguistics.

Author Index

Association for Computational Linguistics
209 N. Eighth Street
Stroudsburg, Pennsylvania 18360

ISBN 978-1-7138-9060-7

CURRAN ASSOCIATES INC.
proceedings.com

Towards Digital Language Equality Workshop (TDLE 2022)

Held at LREC 2022

Marseille, France
20 – 25 June 2022